Essential
Ghent

by André de Swaef

André de Swaef has worked for many
years as a tourist guide in the centre of
Ghent. He is currently attached to the
Historic Monuments Office and organises
'walking dinners' through the city.

*Above: view of the three towers on the Ghent skyline:
St Niklaaskerk, Belfort and St Baafskathedraal*

AA Publishing

Above: *bandstand in the Citadelpark*

Front cover: *Kuip van Gent; Leie riverside; Kwak beer glass.*
Back cover: *Belgian chocolates*

Author: André de Swaef
Translated from the Dutch by: Mary Boorman
© 2000 Kosmos-Z&K Uitgevers B.V., Utrecht
Typesetting: Studio Imago,
Jacqueline Bronsema, Amersfoort
© Automobile Association Developments Limited 2000
© Maps: Bert Stamkot, Cartografisch Bureau MAP,
Amsterdam
First edition

English language edition produced for AA Publishing by:
g-and-w PUBLISHING, Oxfordshire, UK

A CIP catalogue record for this book is available from the
British Library
ISBN 0 7495 3193 2

Kosmos-Z&K publishers make every effort to ensure that
their travel guides are as up-to-date as possible.
Circumstances, however, are very changeable. Opening
times and prices change, and roads are built or closed.
Therefore, Kosmos-Z&K publishers do not accept liability for
any incorrect or obsolete information. Assessments of
attractions, hotels, restaurants and so forth are based upon
the author's own experience and, therefore, descriptions
given in this guide necessarily contain an element of
subjective opinion which may not reflect the publisher's
opinion or dictate a reader's own experience on another
occasion.
   We have tried to ensure accuracy in this guide, but
things do change and we would be grateful if readers
would advise us of any inaccuracies they may encounter.

English language edition published by AA Publishing, a
trading name of Automobile Association Developments
Limited, whose registered office is Norfolk House,
Priestley Road, Basingstoke, Hampshire, RG24 9NY.
Registered number 1878835.

Printed and bound in Italy by Printer Trento srl

Find out more about AA Publishing and the wide range of services the AA provides by visiting our web site at www.theAA.com

Contents

About this Book

KEY TO SYMBOLS

- ✚ map reference to the maps found in the What to See section
- ✉ address or location
- ☎ telephone number
- ⏰ opening times
- 🍴 restaurant or café on premises or near by
- Ⓜ nearest underground train station
- 🚍 nearest bus/tram route
- 🚆 nearest overground train station

- ⛴ ferry crossings and boat excursions
- ✈ travel by air
- ℹ tourist information
- ♿ facilities for visitors with disabilities
- ✋ admission charge
- ↔ other places of interest near by
- ❓ other practical information
- ➤ indicates the page where you will find a fuller description

---

Essential *Ghent* is divided into five sections to cover the most important aspects of your visit to Ghent.

Viewing Ghent pages 5–14
> An introduction to Ghent by the author
> Ghent's Features
> Essence of Ghent
> The Shaping of Ghent
> Peace and Quiet
> Ghent's Famous

Top Ten pages 15–26
The author's choice of the Top Ten places to see in Ghent, listed in alphabetical order, each with practical information.

What to See pages 27–90
The four main areas of Ghent, each with its own brief introduction and an alphabetical listing of the main attractions.
> Practical information
> Snippets of 'Did you know…' information
> 5 suggested walks
> 4 suggested drives
> 2 features

Where To… pages 91–116
Detailed listings of the best places to eat, stay, shop, take the children and be entertained.

Practical Matters pages 117–124
A highly visual section containing essential travel information.

Maps
All map references are to the individual maps found in the What to See section of this guide.
For example, the Boekentoren has the reference ✚ 30B2 – indicating the page on which the map is located and the grid square in which the Boekentoren is to be found. A list of the maps that have been used in this travel guide can be found in the index.

Prices
Where appropriate, an indication of the cost of an establishment is given by **£** signs:
£££ denotes higher prices, **££** denotes average prices, while **£** denotes lower charges.

Star Ratings
Most of the places described in this book have been given a separate rating:

- ✪✪✪ Do not miss
- ✪✪ Highly recommended
- ✪ Worth seeing

Viewing Ghent

Above: *aerial view of the city*
Right: *'head in the noose'*
signboard

André de Swaef's Ghent

Is Ghent Safe?
It is impossible to imagine the streets of Ghent without the police. The city centre is a car-free zone so the police in that area use bicycles. The strong police presence is a preventative and should not be seen as an indication of the level of crime.

Some historic towns have become open-air museums – but not Ghent. Here periods of history merge seamlessly. The residents of Ghent do not simply live in the past but are open to modern ideas.

Ghent locals are fond of talking, arguing and discussing. The topic doesn't matter: art, politics or the awful weather, the visitor to Ghent just cannot avoid a good discussion. The locals are steeped in a centuries-old tradition of stubbornness. Whether the subject is something everyday or the deeper meaning of life – words rule.

Ghent is a hospitable city and there are plenty of places where you can daydream in peace about other countries. You can drink tea in Turkishtown, feast on Spanish tapas and dance the tango in a Latin American bar. Once you have finished eating you can carry on into the small hours before the barman finally shuts the door.

If you are spending time in Ghent during the winter, be sure to wear a thick overcoat. Wrap up warm against the chilly afternoon and wander through the streets of the town. You may experience a feeling of melancholy and wistfulness and surrendering to it might just result in a fondness for the place.

The police in the city centre use bicycles as a means of transport: fast and environmentally friendly

Ghent in Figures

Geography
• Area: 15,642 hectares

Population
• Total population 250,000 of whom 8 percent are from ethnic minorities.

Historic buildings
Ghent, with 1,400 years of history, is the city with the largest number of listed buildings in Belgium.
• Medieval castles: 2
• Abbeys: 5
• Begijnhofs (▶ 24, panel): 3
• Churches: 59
• Museums: 19

Exhibitions, fairs and markets
• Exhibitions: 61
• Fairs: 38
• Markets: 24

Library
• 32 percent of the population of Ghent has a library ticket, which means they read more books than any other Belgians.

Trams and buses
• Tram and bus routes: 98
The tram is held up 513 times a year by accidents or a vehicle parked on the lines.

The tram is a mobile advertisement hoarding and the best means of transport in the city centre

Miscellaneous
• 3,000 gravestones vanish every year.
• There are 300,000 trees, 165kg of weed-killer is used annually and only 25 percent of the well water is drinkable. Working on the internet has reduced the amount of paper used by the city council by only 330,000 sheets a year.
• Foreign visitors to conferences spend four times the amount of the average tourist and a Japanese tourist spends about 12,000 Belgian francs per day.
• 20,000 new students enrol each year in the University of Ghent
• There are 500 recognised sports clubs, 3 cinemas, 8 swimming pools, 85 places of worship for 17 different faith communities.
• One man from Ghent has been into space.
• Average annual consumption of beer is 114 litres per head.

Multicultural City
The multicultural character of Ghent is striking. It is not clear how many members of ethnic minorities are living in the city, legally or illegally. Yet the city council is regularly at loggerheads with the central government over deportation of foreigners, sometimes to the great annoyance of the central government. Romanian gypsies in particular have found their way to Ghent.

Ghent's Features

It sometimes seems that Ghent itself is unaware of its own character and attraction as a tourist destination. You would think that a city boasting the largest number of listed buildings in Belgium would play a bigger part in the tourism industry than it does. However, the local people seem to take their beautiful buildings for granted and this is precisely what gives Ghent its charm and ensures that there is life everywhere. In order to discover what makes the city unique you really need to explore it on foot. That way you will get the most from Ghent's beautiful historic buildings and you won't miss anything that happens on the spur of the moment. Just when you least expect it, something interesting seems to be going on in a little square tucked away in the back streets.

The slaughterhouses of the meat market are now flower stalls and stands selling chips

THE 10 ESSENTIALS

*If you have only a short time to visit Ghent and
would like to attempt a really complete picture
of the city, here are the essentials.*

The fish market in Ghent

• **Look at Gravensteen through the eyes of a child**, daydream about knights and shudder at the instruments of torture (▶ 18).

• **Stroll round one of the many markets** that are held here and there in the city between Friday morning and Sunday afternoon.

• Stop at a chocolate shop and **sample the famous Belgian chocolates**; real Ghent chocolates are made by Daskalides.

• **Climb a church tower or bell tower** and enjoy the view.

• **Visit the Kinderen Alynshospitaal**, a medieval place of worship that now houses the Museum voor Volkskunde (▶ 43).

• **Take a boat trip round the Ghent basin** and see the guild houses on the Graslei as well as the idyllic Lieve canal (▶ 20).

• Discover six centuries of painting and visit **The Adoration of the Mystic Lamb** (▶ 16) as well as **S.M.A.K.** (▶ 25), with works from the Flemish primitives to post-modernists.

• **Go on a pub crawl** and taste a number of Belgian beers (▶ 98–9, 101).

• Treat yourself to a **special meal in the Patershol**, a medieval labyrinth in the heart of the city (▶ 21).

• Go to an event or a performance in the **Vooruit Arts Centre** and discuss it over a drink in the foyer (▶ 71).

Shiver whilst looking at thumbscrews, a guillotine, hatchets and other executioner's tools

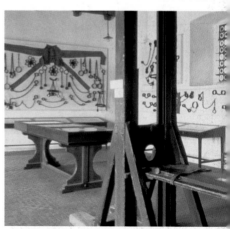

The Shaping of Ghent

630
St Amand, a French missionary, founds abbeys on the River Leie at Ganda (▶ 60), a celtic word meaning 'river confluence'. The city of Ghent grows up around these abbeys.

879–83
The Normans erect their tents near Ghent.

1180
Philip of Alsace commissions the building of the Gravensteen.

1251
The Lieve canal is dug and Ghent becomes an important port.

1300
With a population of

The statue of Emperor Charles V on the Prinsenhof, where he was born

60,000 Ghent is the second largest city north of the Alps, after Paris.

1338
During the Hundred Years War Jacob van Artevelde sides with England so that the import of sheep's wool for the cloth industry can continue.

1381
Jacob van Artevelde is murdered during a weavers' uprising.

1382
After a fierce battle at Westrozebeke the city

has to struggle with a shortage of men.

1500
Emperor Charles V born in the Prinsenhof.

1538
The people of Ghent rise up because they no longer want to pay taxes to Charles V to fund the war.

1547
Ghent's connection with the North Sea improves with the construction of the Sassevaart.

1561
Ghent becomes a diocese.

1566
Iconoclasts plunder and destroy Catholic buildings.

St Baafsabdij, founded by St Amand in 630

1576
Pacification of Ghent. The persecution of heretics is abolished.

1577–84
Ghent becomes a Calvinist republic.

1584
Alexander Farnese reintroduces Catholicism with a heavy hand and 10,000 people flee to the Northern Netherlands.

1667
Appearance of *Ghendsche Post Tydinghe*, one of the first Dutch-language newspapers, which was prohibitively expensive.

1800
Lieve Bauwens smuggles machines from England. Ghent becomes an industrial city with a lot of child labour and social exploitation and earns itself the nickname 'Little Manchester'.

1814
The United States and England conclude their war and sign a peace treaty in Ghent.

1815
On his flight from Napoleon, Louis XVIII of France spends one hundred days in Ghent.

1817
William I founds the University of Ghent.

1820
After centuries of war and the plague, Ghent again reaches the level of population it had in 1300: 60,000.

1830
The Belgian state is founded, but Ghent hopes to be affiliated to The Netherlands.

1886
In the struggle for the maintenance of the Dutch language, the Royal Flemish Academy of Language and Literature is founded.

1890
Exploited workers make their voices heard. Their foreman Eduard Anseele is a friend of Emile Zola. Ghent becomes a hotbed of socialism.

1913
Ghent World Fair. Jack Daniels whiskey wins a gold medal.

1930
University of Ghent becomes Dutch speaking.

1977
Ghent merges with its ten satellites: Afsnee, Drongen, Gentbrugge, Ledeberg, Mariakerke, Oostakker, St Amandsberg, St Denijs-Westrem, Wondelgem and Zwijnaarde.

1998
The citizens of Ghent are the first people in Belgium to compel a referendum on a local issue (▶ 70).

1999
According to certain criteria, Ghent is the most densely populated city in the world.

2000
The world indoor athletics championships are organised in Blaarmeersen. The largest flower basket in history is hung on the E. Braunplein.

Jacob van Artevelde gave his name to the Arteveldestad

Peace & Quiet

A beautiful fountain in the Koning Albertpark

Hassle, stress and pressure are unknown concepts in Ghent and you never have to go far to find peace and quiet. The city even has a stretch of natural landscape, the Bourgoyen-Ossemeersen, situated within the built-up area.

Bourgoyen-Ossemeersen

Between the ring canal and the ring road there is a nature reserve covering 200ha which is so well hidden behind rows of houses that even many local people do not suspect its existence. It consists of grassland, most of which is under water during winter. Many waders and waterfowl are seen here over the winter and if you have the time you can watch from one of the two hides and tick off the birds you see on the lists provided for the ongoing record: herons, little grebes, ducks in all shapes and sizes, coots, widgeon, moorhens, teal and swans. In spring a number of species nest here including curlews, lapwings, great crested grebes and snipe, and weasels and stoats breed in the dry areas. There is excellent skating to be enjoyed if there has been a hard frost after heavy rain.

This natural area was used for the Ghent World Fair of 1913 and visitors could take a trip along the showpiece section of Belgian Railways. You can now walk along the line of the old railway but you must keep to the footpath. It takes you along a former arm of the River Leie and the Valkenhuishoeve, a farmhouse built in 1624. Guided walks are organised for those who would like to know more about the fauna and flora. For more information, enquire at De Grutto, the visitors' centre situated in Gandhistraat.

Citadelpark

Going for a walk in the Citadelpark (➤ 37) in the south of the city is a Ghent tradition and is part of a visit to Ghent. You don't have to walk; you can just sit on a bench and watch the world go by. Like every park, this one has its well-loved and familiar characters, from the old ladies who feed the ducks to people walking their dogs. Waterfalls, rockeries, hilly areas, carpets of flowers and statues create the atmosphere of an English garden. For example, there is the well-known sculpture *The Prisoners* by Jules Lagae. But the words peace and quiet certainly apply here because this is the home of the Museum voor Schone Kunsten (Museum of Fine Art ➤ 53) and Stedelijk Museum voor Aktuele Kunst (Museum of Contemporary Art ➤ 25). The Kuipke (➤ 47), a large hall, part of which was once destined for the Belgian Congo, stands in the middle of the park. It is now used for rock concerts and the six-day cycling championships also take place there. The calls for an underground car park to be built here are getting ever louder.

Citadelpark: hectares of rest and relaxation

Other peaceful places in the centre

The Koning Albertpark (➤ 46), close to the nerve centre of the public transport system, is an ideal place to find peace and relaxation among its fountains, wide footpaths, beautiful trees and flowers. The two begijnhofs, Elisabethbegijnhof (➤ 24) and the Begijnhof Onze-Lieve-Vrouw Ter Hove (➤ 32) are amazingly quiet places. If you are looking for silence and at the same time want to enjoy beautiful flowers, the Botanical Garden (➤ 34) is a must.

Ghent's Famous

Jacob van Artevelde

Jacob van Artevelde (1290–1345), an aristocrat, sided with England during the Hundred Years War in order to protect the city's most important livelihood, the cloth industry. The people of Ghent have a great affection for this 'Protector of Flanders' and they still refer to the city as 'Arteveldestad'.

John of Gaunt

John of Gaunt (Jan van Gent 1341–99) was the fourth son of Edward III and was born in the St Baafsabdij (▶ 60) during the Hundred Years War. He later became Duke of Lancaster. He has lent his name to a bird: the northern gannet is called *Jan van Gent* in Dutch.

Statue of Jan Palfijn. The forceps that he patented are on exhibition in the Museum voor Volkskunde.

Hugo van der Goes

Hugo van der Goes (1440–82) is one of the most important modernisers in painting. He painted the *Portinari Altar*, which now hangs in the Uffizi gallery in Florence. The house in St Pietersnieuwstraat where the huge canvas was painted bears a brass plaque.

Charles V

Charles V (1500–58), at the age of 16, became ruler of an empire on which 'the sun never set'. He had many mistresses and is said to have fathered at least 57 illegitimate children. Charles V ruled the Burgundian Netherlands, Spain, the Austrian inheritance, the Holy Roman Empire, and Central and South America. Thousands of non-Catholics lost their lives because of his religious zeal.

Maurice Maeterlinck
Maurice Maeterlinck (1862–1949) received the Nobel Prize for literature in 1911. His play *Pelléas et Mélisande* was set to music by Debussy and *De Blauwe Vogel* (*The Bluebird*) was filmed twice, once with Shirley Temple.

Jan Palfijn

Jan Palfijn (1650–1730) established himself in Ghent as a surgeon. Although most of them do not know his name his invention of the obstetric forceps has alleviated pain for countless women in childbirth.

Joseph Plateau

Several years before he became blind Joseph Plateau (1801–83) discovered that a rapid succession of still images would produce a moving picture. As an originator of the cinema he gave his name to the trophy that is awarded annually at the Film Festival of Flanders.

Top Ten

Above: a beautiful view of the old
city centre from St Michielsbrug
Right: the Bellman, the town crier
of Ghent

1
The Ghent Altarpiece

✠ 30B3–31A3

✉ St Baafskathedraal; St Baafsplein

🕐 Apr–Oct: daily. 9:30–12 and 2–6; Nov–Mar: daily. 10:30–12 and 2:30–4. Closed in the morning on Sundays and feast days

🍴 Restaurants on Braunplein and St Baafsplein (££)

🚌 Bus 16, 17, 18, 19, 38; tram 21, 22, 40, 41, 42

♿ Very Good

✋ Expensive

*This masterpiece by the two Van Eycks,
Hubert and Jan, is better known as*
The Adoration of the Mystic Lamb, *a name
that refers to the subject of the central panel.*

In 1420 the churchwarden and alderman of Ghent, Joos Vijd, together with his wife Elisabeth Borluut, gave Hubert van Eyck the commission to paint an altarpiece or reredos (a decorated panel behind an altar). When the artist died in 1426 his brother Jan took over the brush and in 1432 he completed an absolute pinnacle in art history. *The Adoration of the Mystic Lamb* consists of 20 panels, a symphony in colour, the ultimate synthesis of medieval painting and a foretaste of what was going to develop subsequently in the art of northwestern Europe. First the van Eycks regarded colour composition as extremely important, and second we have in front of us the first example of a painting in oils. The van Eycks perfected the type of paint which is a mixture of linseed oil, egg yolk and turpentine. The painting technique is responsible for the warm glow from the surface of the canvas. *The Adoration of the Mystic Lamb* was painted on smooth oak panels, the foundation consists of a layer of white paint that reflects and scatters the light. We see flowers and trees from the four winds, exotic items, villages and Gothic churches. The impeccable skill displayed enables the viewer to identify all the different types of wood and precious metals in the painting. The detail is so fine that you can make out every hair in the hairstyles. Examination under the microscope has revealed that even blood vessels are visible, the incidence of light is conveyed logically, and in the drops of water from the fountain you can see the reflection of the surroundings! Not for nothing is this masterpiece called the conquest of realism. We also see the misty landscape that we later encounter in Leonardo da Vinci's work, an early form of pointillism, chiaroscuro and feeling for perspective, which was very advanced for the time.

The canvas was hidden from the iconoclasts. It was taken to Paris in 1794 by French revolutionaries. In the 19th century a number of panels ended up in Berlin and the Nazis hid them in a slate mine in Austria together with the rest of their looted works of art. The travels of *The Adoration of the Mystic Lamb* are still not at an end. In 1934 two panels were stolen. only one was recovered.

On his deathbed a certain Arsène Goedertier wanted to divulge the whereabouts of the missing panel but after the words 'key' and 'little cupboard' he breathed his last. The panel is still being sought. Some people think it is concealed in the cathedral itself. If you should come across it, remember that in 1943 ten million Belgian francs was offered for it.

The triptych originally stood in the Vijd Chapel but to protect it from the damaging breath of thousands of visitors and the itchy fingers of potential thieves it has been moved to another location in St Baafskathedraal. It is contained in a glass case with a concrete cage round it that would even protect the canvas should an aircraft crash on to the cathedral.

The Adoration of the Mystic Lamb, *highpoint in the history of art, an explosion of light and colour*

2
Gravensteen

30B4

St Veerleplein 11

09-2259306

Apr–Sep: daily 9–6;
Oct–Mar: daily 9–5

Some restaurants on St
Veerleplein (££)

Tram 1, 10, 11, 13, 40,
42

None

Cheap

Concerts take place
from time to time

*Ghent is not the only place with a castle like
the Gravensteen, there is also one in Syria,
but that is twelve times larger.*

In 1180 Philip of Alsace, inspired by a castle he had seen in the Holy Land, had the Gravensteen built with walls 1.7m thick. It was the largest fortress in the world situated in the centre of a city. One side of the castle was protected by the Leie river.

Initially the Counts of Flanders lived here, but in the 15th century they looked for a better and warmer residence. After that the castle did duty as a mint, court of law and prison. Many people were martyred here during the witch-hunts as you will see from the collection of instruments of torture. The guillotine was last used to behead someone as late as 1861. Parts of the building

were then converted into a textile factory with the result that it soon fell into disrepair. Restoration was carried out from 1894, and fortunately the Ghent World Fair of 1913 provided a good reason for completing the thorough renovation of the Gravensteen.

Castles usually conjure up pictures of valiant knights who repel attacks by the invaders. This fortress served to keep down the unruly local population and it was only ever overrun by the inhabitants of Ghent themselves, notably in 1948 during a student uprising in protest at an increase in the price of beer. In 1999 an unknown person broke in and stole the display of weapons. The following day this collection was found on the doorstep of the police station; the thief had simply wanted to show that security in the Gravensteen left something to be desired.

3
Kerkhof
Campo Santo

*"You only die once.
Only a sausage has two ends."*
– Local saying

Campo Santo has become the product of an ideological battle between various cemeteries in Ghent, including rivalry with the 'beggar's graveyard' as the Westerbegraafplaats is known. The nickname says it all – this is the resting place of the unbelievers: socialists and agnostics. For years there was fierce competition between Campo Santo and the Westerbegraafplaats (▶ 75). Both cemeteries wanted to bury as many famous people as possible and to have the most elaborate monuments.

Several writers, artists and composers are buried at Campo Santo. The location is beautiful: a hill on which Saint Amand would have preached in the 7th century, with a late-baroque chapel at the highest point and trees that were already there when the first burials took place in 1847. This is the last resting place of the cultural, financial and Catholic elite of Ghent; they lie under expensive monuments, 120 of which are listed. Well-known people include man of letters Jan Frans Willems (section A), author Filip de Pilecyn (section A), graphic artist Frans Masereel (section A), writer Rosalie Loveling (section C), poet Karel van de Woestijne and his brother Gustaaf the painter (section F) and a winner of the Nobel Prize for Medicine, Corneel Heymans (section V).

✚ Not on the map

✉ Antwerpsesteenweg

🕓 Daily 10–6

🍴 Chip shops and snack bars near the station (£)

🚌 70–74; 76–78

🚉 Gent-Dampoort Station

♿ None

✋ Free

Opposite: *the keep of the Gravensteen with the flags of the crusaders*

Many artists and poets are buried at Campo Santo

4
Kuip van Gent

✝ 30B3

✉ Korenlei/Graslei

☎ 09–2238853/
09–2243233

🕐 Apr–Nov: daily 10–7.
Evening cruises during
Ghent festivals;
Dec–Mar: advance
booking needed

🍴 Restaurants
on the Graslei (££)

🚌 Tram 1, 10, 11, 41

♿ Good

✋ Moderate

🚢 Bootjes van Gent/
Benelux

❓ Cocktail cruises on
request

*This is the medieval port area of the city,
with magnificent guild houses and charming
views of the historic city.*

The Kuip van Gent, the Ghent basin, includes the part of
the River Leie that flows through the city centre and the
Lieve canal. A 40-minute boat trip takes you past the silent
evidence of ten turbulent centuries. The best introduction
to the city is to look at the Graslei with its medieval guild
houses and the oldest stepped gable in the whole of the
Low Countries, indisputably one of the most beautiful
cityscapes in Europe. Until 1827 the skippers used to
unload corn here. The worthies of Ghent built their five-
storey houses higher than elsewhere, earning the city the
nickname of 'Manhattan of the 13th century'. You sail
under small swing bridges into the 19th century: the grey
district where men, women and children were worked to
death cotton spinning, soap boiling and weaving. This is
the route the fishermen took to the fish market with their
catch and where beer deliveries reached the beer quay. It
is said that the city's monks regularly visited the port by
night, in their small
boats. Once there
they picked up ladies
of the night and
loaded the boats with
barrels of wine. From
the Onthoofdingsbrug
('beheading bridge')
miscreants could get
their last glimpse of
the traders taking
their goods to
Damme. Next, the
Gravensteen comes
into view and you
reach the Lieve, with
its weeping willows
along the bank. At the
end of the tour you

*Enjoy the beautiful
surroundings from a boat
on the Leie*

see Rabot, a textbook example of military construction
from the 15th century and almost the only part that
remains of the original 14km of the city wall.

Two boat firms operate in the Ghent basin: 'Bootjes van
Gent' and 'Benelux', but remember that the covered boats
are too big to go under the small bridges of the Lieve which
means you will miss the most picturesque section.

5
Patershol

In the past the Patershol was not a pleasant place to visit. Nowadays you can have a splendid meal in one of the many restaurants.

Wonderful smells come from the restaurants in the narrow streets of the Patershol

Surrounded by Lange Steenstraat, Geldmunt, Kraanlei and Sluizieken the Patershol is virtually an island in the city. It is a small maze of narrow 12th-century streets, scarcely wide enough for a car, where the cobblestones shine after the rain. Over the years these streets have been occupied by all levels of society: tanners, rich city magistrates, artists and priests. The gloomy, unlit alleyways inspired the Ghent author Jean Ray to write horror stories which were later made into films. Artists such as Frans Masereel and Georges Minne came here to drink beer. Hundreds of workers' families were packed into the district at the beginning of the 20th century with cholera and other epidemics occurring as a result. Sailors came ashore here and looked for the amusement that they had missed while at sea. The Patershol was, for a long time, the haunt of prostitutes and pimps, hooligans and idlers. They had taken over four hectares of the city and made it into a no-go area for the police. Mie Nekkenbijter ('neck-biter') was a lady of easy virtue who speaks most strongly to the imagination. She gave her clients a love bite on the neck as a trade mark sign to their spouses.

Nowadays the Patershol is safer and cleaner than it once was. The estate agents have understood the unique character of the area, renovating the small houses to provide expensive, but attractive dwellings. Many restaurants have opened in this culinary district, known beyond the frontiers of the country, where you can sample everything, from prawns to a typical Flemish casserole.

✚ 30B4

✉ Easiest access along Kraanlei

🍴 First class restaurants (£££)

🚌 Tram 40, 42; bus 55, 57, 58, 69

♿ Few

21

6
Prinsenhof

Many architects live in the neighbourhood of the Prinsenhof

Wander through a virtual castle where the Emperor Charles V was born and Maximilian of Austria spent his honeymoon.

✚ 30B4

✉ Gewad, St Antoniuskaai, Prinsenhof, Lievekaai and the the narrow streets in between

🍴 Restaurants on St Veerleplein (££)

🚌 Tram 1, 10, 11, 13

♿ Good

In the 13th century the Counts of Flanders were already living in the huge castle known as 'Prinsenhof'. It had more than 300 rooms, a pleasure garden and a zoo and became the refuge of Maria de Medici, widow of the French King Henri IV. This area is known to Ghent residents as the place where the Emperor Charles V first saw the light of day on 24 February 1500. His statue, a gift from the Spanish city of Toledo, stands on the peaceful central square, near the only part of the castle still standing, the Donkere Poort. In the 19th century many textile factories, breweries and soap works were established in the rooms of the castle which contributed to the rapid decline of the building. The people who live here now each have a small remnant of the castle in their back gardens and enjoy a calm and peaceful neighbourhood. A model shows what the castle used to look like and helps to fuel your imagination, whilst the fairytale exteriors of some of the buildings transport you to another time. The mix of architectural styles makes this area more than worth a visit. On the one hand there are the castle remains, on the other a mixture of hidden workers' cottages and ultra modern houses. Furthermore, many present-day architects who have designed their own houses live here.

7

St Baafskathedraal

*'Channels of light!
Walkways, staircases, thrones!
Halls of being!'*
−Rainer Maria Rilke after a visit
to the cathedral.

✚	30B3 – 31A3
✉	St Baafsplein
🕐	Daily 7:30–7:15. Closed Sun mornings and feast days
🍴	Restaurants on St Baafsplein (££)
🚌	Bus 16, 17, 18, 19, 38; tram 21, 22, 40, 41, 42
♿	None
✋	Free
❓	Sometimes classical music performances

The cathedral is more than simply the home of *The Adoration of the Mystic Lamb* (► 16). In 942 a parish church, the oldest in Ghent, sat on this spot. It grew continuously and eventually reached its present magnificent form in 1628. Overtime its appearance has changed regularly; a result of fire damage and the destructive mania of the iconoclasts. The Emperor Charles V was baptised here and he invested heavily in the cathedral to make it a fitting place for the celebration of his coronation. The 27 chapels in which saints are honoured also contain the mausoleums of bishops and Catholic patrons. The crypt, with its 15th-century wall paintings, is among one of the largest in Europe and traces of the original building work can still be seen.

The first of the innumerable works of art, the 15th-century Calvary triptych by an unknown master, is in the first side chapel on the right. The Gothic side aisles, flamboyant rococo pulpit, baroque painting *The Conversion of St Bavo* by Pieter Paul Rubens (St Sebastiaans-kapel) and the nave in late Brabant Gothic style give the visitor a thrilling overview of the styles that were able to develop under the auspices of the church. The 5-tonne bell hangs high up in the cathedral but unfortunately it is only possible to climb up the 82m-high tower during the Ghent Festival, held at the end of July. For many local people counting the steps in the tower is an annual tradition.

People look very insignificant next to this huge cathedral

8
St Elisabethbegijnhof

Begijnhof
The *begijnhof*, or *béguinage*, is a community of lay sisters living together within a town – a cross between a convent and an almshouse complex. The history of the begijnhofs goes back to the 12th century and they were especially prevalent in Belgium, Germany and The Netherlands.

The lay sisters no longer live here but the feeling of peace remains

Thirteen Flemish begijnhofs have appeared on the UNESCO list of World Heritage Sites since 1998. A year later the committee decided to include 24 Flemish bell towers.

After the crusades there was a surplus of women in the large cities who, because of a feeling of insecurity and loneliness, sought each other's company. As lay sisters they occupied themselves with creating and selling needlework. This is one of the theories for the origin of the begijnhofs. There are scarcely any sisters left nowadays but their residences, or begijnhofs, are listed buildings and provide an oasis of peace in the heart of the city.

 30A4

 The area between Rabotstraat and Begijnhoflaan

 Snack bars in the Brugse Poort (£)

 Tram 1, 10, 11, 13; bus 16, 17, 18, 19, 38, 65

 Good

 Free

 Must be quiet

The St Elisabethbegijnhof was founded in 1242 by Countess Johanna of Constantinople. Part of its original character was lost after a fire in 1674 and the realignment of the streets. The picturesque Proveniersterstraat is a reminder of this past. The white walls with their green doors recall the Sister Superior who sat in her front garden making lace and the little sister Matteken, who in the 15th century held a conversation here with an image of Christ. The charm of this place lies in the tranquil silence. A sculpture by Georges Minne in memory of the melancholic writer Georges Rodenbach looks down on the sailors who visit the Anglo-Saxon church. Families who want to escape the hustle and bustle of city life now live in the begijnhofs and convents. Children can play in the streets, chasing a ball over the cobblestones, without ever having to look out for passing traffic.

9

Stedelijk Museum voor Aktuele Kunst (S.M.A.K.)

Only tomorrow's art will be more up to the minute than the work exhibited here.

Jan Hoet is a name to conjure with in the art world – he is both feted and reviled. He was the manager of the world-famous exhibition Documenta IX in Kassel and that was right up his street, because he personifies what is typified by contemporary art. He fought for years to achieve such a museum of contemporary art in his own city and in 1999 he achieved it in the shape of S.M.A.K. The former casino has become more than a museum, providing a space where the artist and the visitor can enter into dialogue with each other, without lifeless objects on a wall; where live performances are put on and the artists create their work on the spot. There are even dance parties and events.

In this building you can admire the work of the very finest modern artists: Panamerenko, Joseph Beuys, Francis Bacon, Andy Warhol, Roger Raveel, Pierre Alechinsky, Jan Fabre, Luc Tuymans, Edward Lipski and Johannes Kahrs. These are just a few of those whose work forms part of the vast collection, a collection so large that completely new special exhibitions can be held regularly. In this museum Andy Warhol is an 'Old Master' while the collection is rounded off with names that sound familiar only to insiders in the modern art world.

For everyone, enthusiast or not, S.M.A.K. makes a refreshing change after seeing the Flemish Primitives elsewhere in the city.

30B1

Citadelpark

09–2211703

Tue–Sun 10–6

Restaurant in museum (£££)

Bus 5, 50, 53, 58, 76; tram 12, 13

Very good

Very expensive

Reserve a guided tour in writing: fax 09–2217109

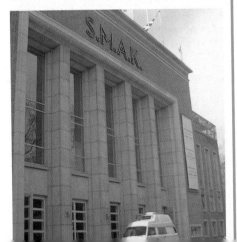

S.M.A.K. was once a casino but is now a museum of modern art

10
Vrijdagmarkt

:heavy_plus_sign: 30B3 – 31A3

:fork_and_knife: Several restaurants ranging from (££) to (£££)

:bus: Bus 5, 16, 17, 18, 19, 50, 52, 68, 69

:wheelchair: Very good

As well as market stalls there are plenty of bars and pavement cafés on the Vrijdagmarkt

The Vrijdagmarkt is an attractive place to sit at a pavement café when you simply want to take a breather.

Large squares the world over are places where demonstrations take place and the Vrijdagmarkt is no exception. On the birth of the Emperor Charles V the square was flooded and frozen forming a huge skating festival took place. This emperor later used the area to organise his book burnings, during which a great deal of Protestant and Calvinist literature went up in flames. His statue once stood here, but today a bronze of Jacob van Artevelde (► 14) proclaims his Roman greeting in the middle of the Vrijdagmarkt.

It was here the guilds fought out their battles, until 1822 it was the place of execution, and since 1199 there have been market stalls in the square. Among the guild houses there is an enormous, eclectic building from 1900, Onze Huis (Our House). This is the headquarters of the socialist workers association and is frequently the place where uprisings begin.

It is worth visiting the Gothic building at number 37, the guild house of the tanners, called Het Toreken. On the edge of the square stands the Dulle Griet (► 36), both a cannon and peace monument. We have the cannonball, which at 340kg flew only a metre, to thank for this paradox. Naturally it has never won a war.

What to See

Above: *horse-drawn carriages*
Right: *sign for 't Velootje, the Penny-Farthing pub*

Ghent

A sign showing the old city towers *and* the technology fair welcomes the visitor off the motorway. Old and new exist side by side in Ghent and that includes the things to see. Romanesque architecture alongside modern buildings, medieval and contemporary art. But you have not visited Ghent properly if you have merely looked, because it is a city in which you must take part too, and there are endless possibilities for enjoying life.

Ghent is actually a big village with the air of a city. The sights are spread out and it can be difficult to get a grip on this capital of East Flanders. But many people who come here for a weekend have lost their hearts to Ghent and some have even settled permanently in the the city.

'In the whole of Christendom there is not a people to be found with the disposition of the citizens of Ghent.'

ERASMUS VAN ROTTERDAM
(1469–1536)

———————●———————

Ghent

What makes Ghent worth visiting are its buildings, either in all their splendour or in a sad state of decay, silent witnesses to a fascinating history. Houses, monuments, churches and abbeys that were there when the European political tide turned. If Ghent's walls could speak, we could spend hours listening to their stories.

Hubert and Jan van Eyck being greeted by the citizens of Ghent

Dante had already warned Philip IV that a terrible revenge awaited him if he annexed Ghent. The Spaniards and the fanatical supporters of the Counter Reformation had to cope with a republican and Calvinistic people, and Napoleon was afraid when he saw the anti-French citizens of Ghent. Even when Belgium became independent in 1830 Ghent was at odds with the state when the citizens of the town went against it and supported the Dutch House of Orange.

The buildings that have survived pollution, wars and urbanisation bear traces of the many artists who expressed their creativity in the city: van Eyck, Hugo van Der Goes, Victor Horta, Maurice Maeterlinck, Georges Minne and many others. The list of artists is growing with the founding of S.M.A.K., the contemporary art museum (▶ 25).

The people of Ghent are proud of their history and they themsleves are well worth listening to; a lively people, opinionated but never boring.

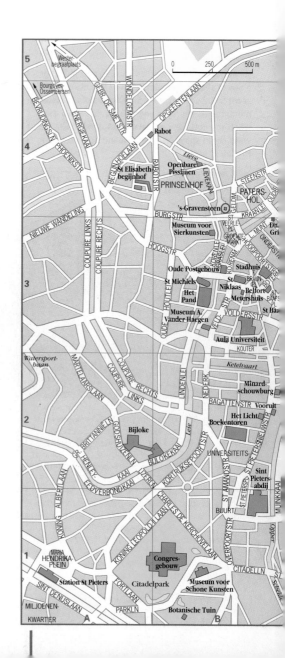

GHENT

TURKISH

TOLHUISLAAN

DOORNZELESTR

Handelsdok

AFRIKALAAN

SLEEPSTRAAT

TOWN

HAM

KONGOSTR

KLEIN
MANCHESTER

TOLLOTGRACHT

BAUDELOKAAI

HAM

DOK ZUID

KOOPVAARDIJLAAN

Achterdok

Campo
Santo

ST AMANDS

DAGM

STEENDAM

NIEUWPOORT

Jacobs

ANTWERPSE STEENWEG

BERG
LAND VAN WAASLAAN

DAMPOORTSTR

SCHOOLKAAI

VERKAAI

OUDE
BEESTENM

St Baafs-
abdij

Station
Dampoort

Groot
Begijnhof

WITTEMOLENSTR

de Duivel-
steen

REEP

BISDOM-
PL

GANDASTR

KASTEELLAAN

DENDERMONDSE

RABANT

DAM

KEIZER KAREL STR

F. LOUISBERGKAAI

Brusselses

ST ANNA-
PLEIN

KUIPERSK

HERNIS

STEENWEG

WILSONPL

TOEKOMSTSTR

FRANKLIN ROOSEVELTLN

Koning Albertpark

TWEEBRUGGENSTR

FORELSTR

LAAN

WOLTERSLAAN

F. LOUSBERGKAAI

Rietvinck

Klein
Begijnhof

Schelde

Bernard-
park

VLAAMSEKAAI

G. CALLIERLN

ZUIDERPARKLAAN

KERKSTRAAT

GENTBRUGGE

TENTOONSTELL

Het Strop

OUDE BRUSSELSE

LIEVENSLAAN

van

BELLEVUE

BRUSSELSE STEENWEG

WEG

Afleiding

LEDEBERG

N

A

B

What to See in Ghent

BEGIJNHOF ONZE-LIEVE-VROUW TER HOVE ✪✪✪

+ Not on the map
✉ Lange Violettestraat 209
🕐 Daily until 9PM
🚋 Tram 21, 22, 40, 41, 42
& Good
👆 Free

This gem of a begijnhof, which is included on the UNESCO list, stands well hidden behind walls in the Lange Violetenstraat. The great difference between it and the better known Elisabethbegijnhof (▶ 24) is that the present owners and residents of the former convent have signed a contract undertaking to maintain its peace and quiet. You cannot go in after nine o'clock in the evening and anyone who wants to end their days here had better put their name down on the waiting list straight away. The 17th-century houses and the church – with a painting that points to *The Adoration of the Mystic Lamb* (▶ 16) – are still completely intact. A walk through the grounds gives a view of a Calvary and the abbey of Nieuwen Bosch. You need special permission to visit the house of the Sister Superior.

BELFORT ✪✪✪

+ 30B3
✉ St Baafsplein
🕐 May–Oct: daily 10–5
🚋 Tram 21, 22, 40, 41, 42; bus 16, 17, 18, 19, 38, 3
& Good
👆 Cheap
↔ St Baafskathedraal (▶ 23)

Like the begijnhofs, the Flemish bell towers are on the UNESCO list. The bell towers are symbols of the power and the autonomy of the cities. They were outstanding lookout posts, giving advance warning of attacking troops or hotbeds of revolt. The bells served as an alarm signal so that the populace could mobilise and collect water from the Leie for fire fighting. The golden dragon on the top of the spire is a symbol of the city and weighs so much, at least 400kg, that it failed as a weather vane. This bell tower was only completed in 1913 when it was quickly finished for the World Fair. The cellar of the adjoining Cloth Hall now houses the VVV tourist office (▶ 48).

The 95m-high symbol of an independent city: the bell tower with the golden dragon

BERNARDPARKJE ✪

This once housed the Ghent zoo which has left some traces behind. Although this is the least known and the smallest park in Ghent it is perhaps the quietest and the most attractive. Moreover it is surrounded by the lovely houses of Hertstraat and Hofstraat. Students often come here to study in the peaceful surroundings during examinations, there are ducks swimming on the pond and dogs bring their masters here for a walk.

🚩 31A1
✉ Bernardstraat
🚌 Bus 55, 57, 58, 70, 74, 78
♿ Very good
↔ St Pietersabdij (▶ 65)

Many regard the Bijloke as the nicest museum in Ghent

BIJLOKE MUSEUM ✪✪✪

The Bijloke, on the banks of the Leie and the Coupure canal is a large complex of buildings that was a hospital and hospice, and an abbey in the 14th century. Like many other religious buildings it became a target of the iconoclasts. The whole complex was restored in 1926.

The cluster of buildings are well used and the activities that take place here are very varied. Forensic pathologists carry out investigations into suspicious deaths; an ultra-modern concert hall offers the very peak of pleasure for the lover of classical music and a museum of archaeology and antiquities informs the visitor about the history of the city. A number of architectural elements give a decorative and somewhat fairytale impression.

🚩 30A2
✉ Godshuizenlaan 2
☎ 09–2251106
🕐 Tue–Sun 9:30–5
🚌 Tram 21, 22, 40; bus 14, 15, 65, 69
♿ Good
💷 Moderate
↔ Coupure (▶ 35)

DID YOU KNOW?

When the decision was taken in 1904 to close the Ghent zoo, the animals – including an elephant – were sold at auction. Because no one knew what to do with an elephant the unwieldy animal was sold for a song to a butcher who put it in his sausages.

30B2
Rozier
09–2253330
Mon–Fri 9–6
Bus 5, 50
Few
Free
St Pietersabdij (▶ 65)

The library tower, known as the fourth tower

BOEKENTOREN

Nearly 20,000 students register at the University of Ghent each year and although it has a good reputation the conditions are not ideal. The lecture theatres could do with a couple of coats of paint and if there were more space no one would have to sit on the stairs to hear the lectures. However, the library, known as the fourth tower, is one of the best and was designed by one of Belgium's leading architects, Henry van de Velde. The tower is 64m high, has 26 floors and space for two million books and manuscripts; it even has a billiard hall. This is the place to come if you want to read a newspaper from 1880. As ever, the charm of the catalogue room with the old card-filing system has had to make way for the less romantic computer.

30B1
Karel Lodewijk
Ledeganckstraat 35
09–2645073
Mon–Thu 2–5;
Sat–Sun 9–12
Bus 5, 50
Excellent Free
S.M.A.K. (▶ 25)
Guided tour by arrangement

BOTANICAL GARDEN

Ghent would not be Ghent if the city did not attach great importance to flowers, an importance that goes far beyond the azalea. The study garden of the Faculty of Science is open daily, free of charge, and shows herbs and plants that originate from all over the world. Obviously you will have to visit the hot houses to see the tropical plants. Throughout the seasons, there are boards giving details of where the plants belong in the flora according to area of distribution.

BRON DER GEKNIELDE JONGELINGEN ✪✪

Georges Minne was a distinguished pupil of the sculptor Auguste Robin. Sculptures of slim, naked youths are his trademark and he has made hundreds of variations on the theme. His work has become internationally famous and is found in museums the world over. This circle of naked men is commonly known as *pietjesbak* (pronounced 'peetyes'). It is a play on words because the word can mean either 'dice basin' or 'Pete's basin'. According to local legend, anyone who drinks the water in the fountain will have eternal life. You are probably far more likely to catch something nasty!

> ### DID YOU KNOW?
>
> The biggest complaint of visitors to Ghent concerns the midges. It is claimed that the midges are the most vicious in Europe and they keep people awake at night. This is probably because there is so much still and shaded water about.

COUPURE ✪✪

As an inland port, Ghent has been preoccupied with establishing a good connection with the sea. In the 18th century the Coupure was dug to connect the city with the Bruges–Ostend canal. The quays immediately became places where the burghers and rich industrialists strolled or came to live: simple workers were forbidden to even show themselves here. Many of the burghers' houses are still reflected in the Coupure and the percentage of French-speaking residents is higher here than elsewhere in Ghent. You can wander along the canal admiring the beautiful facades of the houses and soaking up the atmosphere.

➕ 30B3
✉ E. Braunplein
🚍 Tram 21, 22, 40, 41, 42; bus 3, 16, 17, 18, 19, 38
↔ Belfort (➤ 32)

Citadelpark (➤ 13)
➕ 30A/B1
✉ Leopold III-laan, Emile Clauslaan, Ch. de Kerkckhovelaan
🍴 Foyer S.M.A.K. (£££)
🚍 Tram 12, 13; bus 14, 15, 23, 28, 48, 49, 55, 57, 58, 69, 73, 74, 94, 95
🚉 St Pietersstation
♿ Good

Above: *the Fountain of the Kneeling Youths*

➕ 30A2
🚍 Bus 3, 16, 17, 18, 19, 38, 65, 69; tram 21, 22, 40
♿ Good
↔ Bijloke Museum (➤ 33)

➕ 30B3
✉ Grootkanonplein
🚋 Tram 40, 42;
bus 55, 58, 69
↔ Vrijdagsmarkt (▶ 26)

DULLE GRIET ✪

This 15th century cannon makes a strange and somewhat paradoxical choice for a peace monument The Dulle Griet ('Mad Meg') is more than 5m long (until a few years ago the homeless used to sleep in the barrel) and ought to have fired stone cannonballs. But since the balls weighed 340kg apiece they only flew one metre and cracked the canons barrel too. In any case the Dulle Griet has given its name to a local white beer and to one of the best known pubs. There is even a chip shop called 'De Dulle Friet'.

➕ 30B3
✉ Groentenmarkt 5
☎ 09–2334251
🚋 Tram 12, 41
♿ Few
↔ St Veerleplein (▶ 65)

Above: the Dulle Griet is a weapon of war that went wrong, the cannonballs used were too heavy to fly very far

GALGENHUISJE ✪

There is some doubt whether this is the smallest pub in Ghent or not. Whatever the figures, it is certainly tiny and full of atmosphere.

The name refers to the iron hooks that you can still see on the corner with the Vleeshuis. Before being burnt at the stake on the Veerleplein criminals were riveted to these hooks. They were then put to shame by the many visitors to the vegetable market and in this way any potential thieves were warned of the dire consequences of their criminal deeds.

Possibly the smallest pub in Ghent

A Walk to the Citadelpark

De Muink is the district between Koning Albertpark and the Opperschelde and it makes a peaceful approach to the St Pietersabdij and the Citadelpark. Woodrow Wilsonplein is the newest square in the city. Lovely houses perished to make way for a modern administrative centre and a shopping centre.

Turn left by the water on to the Muinkkaai.

From here you have a wonderful view of the monumental entrance to the concert hall of the Vooruit arts centre (► 71).

Turn left into Guldenpoortstraat and immediately take the right turn into Hertstraat.

Hertstraat cuts across a tangle of small streets and alleys, once so typical of industrial Ghent. At the end of this street is the Bernardparkje (► 33), the remains of a zoo, surrounded by chic burghers' houses.

Turn left by Bernardstraat and follow the steep path up the Kantienberg.

Now you are looking down on the back of the vineyards of the St Pietersabdij (► 65), worth a small detour and a visit. Left from the bridge (made out of an industrial container) stands the cinema complex Decascoop, where in October you will see film stars wandering around during the Flanders Film Festival. The Rabot (► 58) and a small piece of wall are remnants of the city walls and you can also see the Boekentoren (► 34) from here. The Kantienberg crosses the Overpoortstraat, the student quarter where many litres of beer flow on Thursday evenings.

Keep straight on and follow the Kunstlaan.

The large building on the right hand side is a military base, where there has not been much activity since conscription was abolished. You are now looking straight into Citadelpark (► 13) which contains the large art museums of the city, the sports complex De Kuipke, the congress centre and the botanical garden (► 34).

Distance
4km

Time
2–6 hours

Start point
W. Wilsonplein
⊞ 31A2

End point
Citadelpark
⊞ 30A/B1

Lunch
Foyer of the S.M.A.K. (££)

Crevices, fissures and caves: the Citadelpark is a nice place to spend time

37

✚ 31A3
✉ Limburgstraat
🚫 No access
🚋 Tram 12, 40, 41, 42
↔ St Baafskathedraal (► 23)

Above: *left the Geeraard de Duivelsteen; right the Nationale Bank*

GEERAARD DE DUIVELSTEEN ⭐⭐

This is a name that fires the imagination but its origin is unclear. It is thought that Geeraard Vilain, after whom the building is named, was probably dark-skinned and so was referred to as 'the devil' (*duivel* is Dutch for devil). It is a beautiful building and also one of the oldest in the city. Unfortunately it is not possible to visit the crypt. This large, dark vault would otherwise have become a great tourist attraction and could certainly have inspired the author Umberto Eco. During the buildings history it has served as a house of correction, a prison, an armoury and an orphanage, and it is now currently in use as the National Archive. For small children it remains a grim castle, perfect as a setting for stories of ghosts and witches.

THE GHENT ALTARPIECE (► 16, TOP TEN)

✚ 30B3
✉ Korenlei 7
🕐 Thu–Tue 11
🚋 Tram 12, 41; bus 3, 16, 17, 18, 19, 38
♿ Few
↔ Kuip van Ghent (► 20)

GILDEHUIS VAN DE ONVRIJE SCHIPPERS ⭐⭐⭐

The *onvrije* ('unfree') skippers were those who did not have the right to sail on the inland waters of Ghent. When the rule was scrapped in 1663 the newly freed skippers built a guild house with great pomp and circumstance to impress their rivals, the 'free' skippers. This rococo facade with the gilded caravel above it dominates the Korenlei and certainly succeeds in its intention. The building became a pub and an inscription notes that food, drink and gifts could be bought there. The tradition has been maintained.

GILDEHUIS VAN DE VRIJE SCHIPPERS ✪✪✪

Vrije ('free') skippers had an absolute monopoly on the part of the River Leie between the two bridges, Grasbrug and St Michielsbrug, and so could easily make a living. They built their guild house in Brabant Gothic. Here and there the architecture shows traces of the unfolding Renaissance, and the arms of Emperor Charles V are carved in the gable: *Plus Oultre*, which roughly translates as 'onward ever onward and upward'. The entrance is decorated with the type of ship which carried Christopher Columbus on his voyages of discovery.

- ✚ 30B3
- ✉ Graslei 14
- 🕐 No access
- 🚋 Tram 12, 41; bus 3, 16, 17, 18, 19, 38
- ↔ Kuip van Ghent (▶ 20)

GILDEHUIS VAN DE WIJNHANDELAARS ✪✪

In 1755, during the time French fashion was followed to the letter all over Europe, this guild house was built for wine merchants in the style of Louis XV. It stands in the part of the harbour where cranes were used, hence Kraanlei, 'Crane Lane'. You can make out the old wine cellars just above the water from the bridge or from a boat. The wine barrels could be taken directly from the boats. On the opposite side of this building was the beer quay; the pub is called Het Waterhuis aan de Bierkant ('The Waterhouse on the Beer-side'), and still has the wooden hatches into the beer cellars. The house is now a Mexican restaurant.

- ✚ 30B4
- ✉ Kleine Vismarkt 2
- ☎ 09–2337151
- 🕐 Daily 11
- 🍴 Pablo's (££)
- 🚋 Tram 1, 10, 11, 13, 40, 42
- ♿ Good
- ↔ Gravensteen (▶ 18)

The guild houses are a meeting place for many young people

GRAVENSTEEN (▶ 18, TOP TEN)

The romantic rear of Jan Breydelstraat can only be admired from a boat

Not on the map
Lievekanaal
Gravensteen (▶ 18)
Bootjes van Ghent (Korenlei)/Benelux (Graslei)

HOUTEN GEVEL (WOODEN FACADES) ●●●

Before a fire in 1490 reduced a large part of Ghent to ashes the city had more than 5,000 wooden houses, painted various colours, mainly with oxblood, and like the houses on the Bosporus built on a slope above the river. In Ghent the positioning had more to do with taxes than aesthetics: taxes on property depended on the height of the building and building at an angle saved many centimetres. There is a wooden facade that has survived the ravages of time and this can be seen in all its glory only from a boat on the Lieve canal. There is an unusual story attached to the colour of this house. The pale yellow of the facade is known officially as 'Isabella' yellow. We have the warlike archduchess of that name to thank for this, after she swore not to wash her underwear until the war was won.

In order to avoid further catastrophes like the fire in 1490 everyone who owned a wooden house had to replace it with a brick one. This was done at the expense of the city, so it is understandable that very few wooden houses are left in Ghent today.

30B3
Anywhere in the basin
None

JAAGPADEN (TOW-PATHS) ●●●

Boats were towed through the canals, using the tow-paths, by horses because the many bridges in the Ghent basin made sailing impossible for vessels with masts. The tow-paths made it possible for the skippers to lower their masts. Some parts of the paths have been preserved and some have even been resurfaced. This has given visitors the opportunity to walk along beside the River Leie.

The best-preserved part of the tow-paths is by the Vleeshuis and from there you can walk to Sleepstraat and beyond. Look out for a wooden beam at the steps by the Grasbrug – this is where the tow-ropes used to be attached.

KERKHOF CAMPO SANTO (▶ 19, TOP TEN)

A Walk from the Church to Socialism

After a quick look in St Niklaaskerk (➤ 61) go into Veldstraat.

Apart from doing some shopping you can feast at the Jewish bakery Bloch, visit Maeterlinck's office and discover some of the lovely houses which are hidden behind neon lights and advertising hoardings. You finally come out by the law courts and the opera house. Many bars here have the grand café atmosphere much prized by opera-lovers all over. On the left of the opera house you can find the Kouter (➤ 47) where a flower market is held each Sunday.

Once you have crossed the water turn left into Ketelvest (➤ 42) and keep straight ahead.

You can walk on the road or on the tow-path alongside the canal. At the end you will see the water of the Muinkschelde which turns and goes underground. It is possible to go by boat under this part of the city. Flor, one of the first restaurants to have an open kitchen, is situated on this bend.

Go back 200m along the Huidervettershoek and turn left by Walpoortstraat.

On the left-hand side there are a number of pleasant pubs and the completely renovated Minard theatre. A little further, past the traffic lights, rises the 'bastion of the socialists', the Vooruit Arts Centre (➤ 71). Enquire whether there is something on during your stay.

Distance
3km

Time
1.5–4 hours

Start point
Korenmarkt
⊞ 30B3

End point
St Pietersnieuwstraat
⊞ 30B2

Lunch
Bloch (£)

This is the church where sailors prayed for protection

30B2

Tram 12, 22

Vooruit (▶ 71)

Above: *it is a pleasure to get lost in the narrow 12th-century streets of the Patershol*

KETELVEST   ✪✪

The most picturesque route from the Vooruit Arts Centre to the Opera house is undoubtedly along the Ketelvest, a canal that was excavated in the 11th century. According to some people it is the foundation of an old city wall that was filled with water. In any case there are different opinions as to the origin of the Ketelvest. Certainly there was a city gate at the end of the canal. You can still feel the dark, oppressive atmosphere as described by authors such as Maeterlinck: the St Barbaracollege, where the future Nobel Prize-winner was educated, is situated on this canal. Behind several 18th-century houses the water flows past a modern cable bridge. The huge stage-sets for operatic productions are taken into the opera house across this bridge.

KINDEREN ALYNSHOSPITAAL ✪✪✪

After the death of two children from the Alyn family in 1354, the Rijm brothers escaped the death penalty by building a place of worship as an act of penance and other buildings followed. The city bought the buildings in 1940 and nowadays they house the Museum voor Volkskunde (Folk Museum) where you can get a glimpse of old trades and crafts. Children love the puppet plays of Pierke Pielarla. Pierke makes jokes in the Ghent dialect for young and old. His name is taken from the famous playwright Luigi Pirandello. In the 'Little Café' in the garden of the old hospital you can drink gin in a pub of the kind that Flanders had by the thousand before World War II. (Some Flemish villages had one pub per seven households.) Recently there seems to have been a change in the museum's policy and sometimes the management puts on thematic exhibitions.

🚻 30B4
✉ Kraanlei 65
☎ 09–2231336
🕐 Tue–Sun 9–5
🚌 Tram 40, 42;
bus 55, 57, 58, 69
♿ Few
🍽 Moderate
🔄 Patershol (▶ 21)

The Kinderen Alynshospitaal is a fascinating and amusing museum

KLEIN-MANCHESTER ✪

This area known as 'little Manchester' is no more than a grey neglected quarter but it is not difficult to evoke the atmosphere of the cotton mills that once stood here by the water. Fortunately the times when women and children laboured 16 hours or more a day are long since past. The buildings are now occupied by squatters, artists make lofts out of former weaving sheds and the decay intensifies. The best way to see the area is to walk along the tow-path from Oudburg or to go on a boat trip.

You can admire the machines from these factories in the Museum voor Industriële Archeologie (Museum of Industrial Archaeology). One item on display is the loom that was used in *Daens,* an Oscar-nominated gritty film based on the novel *Peter Daens* by the local Flemish author Louis Paul Boon.

Bells as big as this sound very loud when rung in the Belfort

KLOKKE ROELAND ✪

The actual Roeland Bell was destroyed by Emperor Charles V when the people of Ghent refused to pay their war taxes. This was no small loss because it meant that they had lost their fire alarm. The proper name for the bell which is now known as the Roeland Bell is 'The Great Triumph' and it was removed from the Belfort in 1914 (► 32). The first attempt to sound the bell electrically caused it to crack. Local school children on visits to the bell are always asked to find the crack. You too can try. On Flemish National Day (11 July), when the Flemish Community Festival takes place, the bells can be heard all over the city; there is a verse about them in the Flemish national anthem which was written by a Ghent man.

A Walk Through Picturesque Little Streets

Take the narrow street at the foot of the cathedral: the Biezekapelstraat.

This is the area for courting par excellence in Ghent, with a view of the beautiful aristocrats house De Sikkel (▶ 58). With luck you will be treated to the sounds of opera, since this building houses the Academy of Music.

Keep straight on.

You come out into an attractive little square: the Zandberg, where local people used to come to fetch water from the pump.

If you take the first street on the left you come into Onderstraat.

You will see the entrance to the Van Ryhovesteen building now housing the City Archaeology Department (▶ 69).

Right opposite the Van Ryhovesteen turn into the narrow Serpentstraat.

As a traveller you will be very welcome in Mosquito Coast, a café where you can consult travel guides from all over the world. Slide evenings and geographical quizzes take place here and, of course, travellers' tales galore are exchanged.

At the end of Sepentstraat turn right.

The monumental rococo facade right in front of you is the Academy of Language and Literature, where, sadly, very little happens. When standing at the entrance to the Academy you are in Koningstraat. Follow it to the end and you arrive in the Vlasmarkt, the epicentre of the Ghent Festivals and the centre of alternative entertainment.

Keep right, avoid the busy St Jacobsnieuwstraat but turn right into Baaisteeg and immediately go left.

Via Ridderstraat and Jan Palfijnstraat walk on to Bisdomkaai. You are in fact walking on an island, but since the channel has been filled in you will hardly notice. There are three buildings on the right; the Nationale Bank that looks more like a Byzantine chapel, the bishop's palace on the opposite side and about 100m further on the house of horror, Geeraard de Duivelsteen (▶ 38).

Distance
2.5km

Time
1–2 hours

Start point
St Baafsplein
✚ 30B3

End point
Lieven Bauwensplein
✚ 31A3

Lunch
Mosquito Coast (££)

The impressive Nationale Bank building

The Koning Albertpark

30B3
St Baafsplein 17
09-2253208
Foyer: daily
Theatre café (££)
Tram 21, 22, 40, 41, 42;
bus 3, 16, 17, 18, 19, 38
Few
Ghent Altarpiece (► 16)

KONINKLIJKE NEDERLANDSE SCHOUWBURG ✪✪

This beautiful building provided a home for the Dutch theatre in strongly 'frenchified' Ghent. It is still the permanent base of the Ghent Dutch Theatre (Nederlands Toneel Gent ► 112). Outside a monument to Jan Frans Willems, founder of the Flemish Movement, watches over the building in all its glory. We see an allegory of a mother suckling her children with the words of the Flemish national anthem and figures from the medieval animal epic *Reynaert de Vos* (*Reynard the Fox*). From the terrace there is a lovely view of St Baafsplein and you can go there for food and drink, although not directly before a performance .

31A2
W. Wilsonplein
Bus 52, 53, 54, 60, 69;
tram 21, 22, 40, 41, 42
Very good
Bernardparkje (► 32)

KONING ALBERTPARK ✪

After the demolition of the railway station in 1928 the bare area between Frère Orbanlaan and Rooseveltlaan was made into a park. There is a corner for young skaters, people with books under their arms walk to and from the nearby city library and certainly in the summer there is a pleasant bustle about the place. Jazz bands come to entertain the office workers who relax here on a bench during their lunch break. In the evening there are regular film showings, sometimes also with live music. The Koning Albertpark is the first and last view many people see of Ghent, as the slip road to the E17 is only 500m further on from the park.

> #### DID YOU KNOW?
>
> According to road maps Ghent lies in the exact centre of Europe, at the intersection of the two most important arteries of communication: the E17 (Stockholm–Lisbon) and the E40 (London–Istanbul).

30B3
Tram 1, 10, 11, 12, 13,
40, 41, 42
Good
St Niklaaskerk (► 61)

KORENMARKT ✪✪

In the 12th-century port city, grain was an important commodity and even now Ghent has one of the biggest grain storage areas in Europe. After the corn had been unloaded and stored in the Spijker (► 66) on the Graslei it was offered for sale in the corn market. Nowadays the square is one of the two nerve centres for trams running to and from St Pietersstation, and one of the best places on sunny days to relax at a pavement café and watch the world go by. Try looking up: the first floor of a pub or shop is more likely than the ground floor to show that this is a beautiful example of a former aristocrats house.

KOUTER ✪

On Sunday mornings people in Ghent go in droves to this square to buy flowers and gulp down a tasty helping of oysters at a seafood stall. Flowers, especially azaleas and begonias, are the pride and trademark of the area and they are celebrated every five years in the huge exhibition *Floraliën*. A flower market has in fact been held here since 1772. It is not surprising that there are sculptures of flower petals all over the Kouter, and if you look carefully you will see the old Dutch name of the flower concealed in the veins. You will recognise all the flowers in the altarpiece *The Adoration of the Mystic Lamb* (► 16).

In addition the Kouter is the last resort for someone looking for a cash machine that still works or for an underground parking space.

SPORTPALEIS DE KUIPKE ✪✪

Without doubt cycling is the Belgian national sport and circuit riding has come into prominence in recent years. This somewhat ordinary sport appeals to young people and, together with judo, is one of the few sports in which Belgium has a chance of winning an Olympic medal. In November the covered circuit at the Kuipke is packed to busting and fanfares encourage the six-day cyclists to victory.

Even if you know very little about cycling but happen to be in the city during the six-day race, don't miss the chance to sit in the central area, drinking beer and cheering on the cyclists. Besides, this is one of the rare opportunities to wander through the concrete catacombs of this monument to cycling history.

Regular techno parties and rock concerts are held to keep the complex profitable. The sport and recreation office will be able to give you the details.

KUIP VAN GHENT (► 20, TOP TEN)

KOUTER
- 30B3
- Tram 21, 22
- Very good
- Ketelvest (► 43)

SPORTPALEIS DE KUIPKE
- 30A/B3
- Citadelpark
- Sport and recreation office: 09–2218071
- For events
- Tram 12, 13; bus 5, 50
- Few
- Variable
- S.M.A.K. (► 25)

Exciting cycling races are held in this building

Cloth is no longer sold in the Cloth Hall but the tourist information office is housed here

LAKENHALLE   ❂❂

During the Middle Ages, Flanders gained the bulk of its wealth from the cloth trade. Buying and selling took place in the cloth halls; goods were sampled and prices discussed. Almost all old Flemish towns have impressive cloth halls. Building work on the Ghent Cloth Hall began too late, in 1425, when the cloth trade was declining in importance. For that reason the building was used for various other purposes; at one time it was a prison. Access to the bell tower is via the Cloth Hall (Belfort ▶ 32).

HET LICHT   ❂❂

No single political party has left so many traces behind in the city as the Socialist Workers' Movement, and even now it seems on Labour Day (1 May) that no one can bring so many majorettes and drummers on to the streets as the Left. The journalists, including Louis Paul Boon, an author nominated for the Nobel Prize, went to the buildings of *Het Licht* (*The Light*) every morning and crouched behind the typewriters. The building, constructed from plans by Fernand Brunfaut in 1930, was restored to its former glory in 1997 and presents a very light facade.

The theatre café, appropriately named 'Backstage', is housed in the building, and nowadays in the adjoining rooms many young girls from Ghent take their first ballet lessons.

➕ 30B2
✉ St Pietersnieuwstraat 129
☎ 09–2333535
⏱ Daily 11
🍴 Restaurant in the building (£)
🚌 Bus 5, 6, 50
♿ Few
↔ Vooruit (▶ 71)

A Walk Round Prinsenhof

A peaceful neighbourhood built on the site of the castle where Emperor Charles V was said to have been born in 1500. You can start off in the Den Tap en den Tepel ('The Tap and Teat') pub by trying some local beers. The proprietor is a fanatical idealist who uses his pub to launch his ideas. At least he usually gets a good hearing after customers have indulged in a number of local beers.

Turn into the Prinsenhof.

There is a statue of Emperor Charles V in the little square and a model of the castle that once stood here. The two towers are all that remain of the Prinsenhof (▶ 22). Next to the towers there are typical workers' cottages which are still lived in.

Walk through the Donkere Poort (Dark Gate) and cross over the Lieve canal.

The military fortification Rabot (▶ 58) is on your right and everywhere there are the ruins of old cotton mills. Many workers died of cancer here at the end of the 19th century.

Turn right and continue to follow the water.

The little *Brug der Keizerlijke Geneugten* is a sculpture by Walter De Buck depicting a number of episodes from the life and legends of Emperor Charles V. A magnificent view of the Lieve canal and the Gravensteen awaits you at the next bridge.

Continue along the Lieve canal on the Lievekaai.

Enjoy the lovely old and modern houses that blend together beautifully here. The author Hugo Claus once lived in the corner house with the stepped gable. The monastery on the opposite side is a place of pilgrimage dedicated to the Blessed Rita (patron saint of expectant mothers), but the cells are let to students. If you continue straight on along St Widowstraat you pass even more wonderful little houses, and you have now come back to your starting point.

Distance
2km

Time
1–2 hours

Start/end point
Gewad
✚ 30B4

Lunch
De Gekroonde Hoofden (££)

The sculpture above the entrance to the Mammelokker

MAMMELOKKER ✪

Mamme in Dutch means 'breast' and *mammelokker* means 'suckling'. When the Cloth Hall (▶ 48) was used as the city jail the small annexe to the Belfort (▶ 32) was the

jailer's house. Above the gateway there is a sculpture of a woman suckling a bearded man. The story behind this image is less erotic than at first appears. The man is Cimon who was condemned to starve to death, but was kept alive by his daughter Pero who came every day to suckle him. The jailers were so touched by this scene that they set the man free.

MANNEKEN PIS ✪

The Manneken Pis, the 17th-century bronze fountain in Brussels, is renowned the world over, both as a piece of sculpture and as a curiosity. It is often forgotten that the oldest Manneken Pis is under the balcony of the town hall at Geraardsbergen, a town south of Ghent. In fact, France has the same statue in bronze and Ghent had a Manneken Pis a century earlier than Brussels. There is a replica over the entrance to the restaurant Het Buikske Vol, but in contrast to many of his fellows he has an empty bladder.

✚ 30B4
✉ Kraanlei 17
☎ 09–2251880
🍴 Buikske vol (££)
↔ Patershol (▶ 21)

Many stories have done the rounds about the origin of Manneken Pis. Most of them can be traced back to the dissolute lives of the Burgundian Flemings. One version is that this could be a hymn of praise to urine that was used to bleach cloth in the Middle Ages and was thus important for trade.

DID YOU KNOW?

The great Ghent industrialist Lieven Bauwens increased his profits by having prisoners work for him. The wood in his factory was delivered by a firm called Sax. The name would have meant nothing to us if the son of the timber merchant had not invented the saxophone.

MARIA HENDRIKAPLEIN ⭐

The first thing you see if you arrive by train, apart from the station designed by Louis Cloquet, is the Maria Hendrikaplein. For four years this square was a building site, but in the spring of 2000 the work was finally completed and the square took on its new look. *Meeting* is the subject of a huge sculpture by Paul van Gijsegem: two bronzes rise from the plinth, symbolising the Leie and the Scheldt rivers. People usually meet each other in this square with its ring of trees, its ice-cream sellers and its comfortable benches.

✚ 30A1
🍴 Snack bars in the station area (£)
🚌 Bus 14, 15, 23, 28, 48, 49, 55, 57, 58, 69, 73, 74, 94, 95; tram 1, 10, 11, 12, 13, 21, 22, 40
♿ Good
↔ Miljoenenkwartier (➤ 52)

METSERSHUIS ⭐⭐⭐

The plans for the guild house for the masons, which had disappeared without trace, have been found in the archives. Because the 16th-century Renaissance house with scrolled gables was so beautiful a copy was built on the Graslei. During restoration work on a house in Cataloniëstraat in the 1980s, a builder found that there was another gable behind the facade: this was the original masons' house. It has now been completely restored and if you compare the copy with the original you will see that the imitators built one storey too many.

The group of statues *Moorish Dancers* stands on top of the Metsershuis. When Emperor Charles V had conquered the Moors in Tunis a dance was introduced into Flanders celebrating this victorious battle. The official sculptor was Walter van Buck, also the founder of the Ghent Festivals, and with luck you will see these images actually move.

✚ Not on the map
✉ Cataloniëstraat 1
🍴 Chez Jean (££)
🚌 Tram 21, 22, 40, 41, 42; bus 3, 16, 17, 18, 19, 38
↔ St Niklaaskerk (➤ 61)

Above: *for many the journey to Ghent begins and ends here: the square in front of St Pietersstation*

51

You can see from the house fronts that the Millionaires' Quarter is proud of its name

30A1
St Pieters-Aalst
Bus 23, 76, 77, 78
Good

MILJOENENKWARTIER ⭐⭐

Near the St Pietersstation, between Krijgslaan and Kortrijksesteenweg there is a fragment of the exhibition site of the Ghent World Fair of 1913. This area exhibited the current art nouveau architecture and after World War I rich citizens added their houses here in the same style. This is how the area got its name of 'Millionaires' Quarter'. It provided perfect publicity for many architects, a wonderful advertisement for their offices, and they have left us an interesting architechtural legacy spanning the period between 1900 and 1950. Advocates, doctors, solicitors and other professionals still live here.

30B2
Walpoortstraat 15
09–2330970
For performances
Vooruit (£)
Bus 5, 6, 50
Good
Variable
Vooruit (► 71)

MINARDSCHOUWBURG ⭐⭐

The architect Louis Minard was an art lover who used his own savings to build a neo-classical theatre. Until the Ghent Dutch Theatre (Nederlands Toneel Gent) was established this was the only place in Ghent where local people could see plays, mainly folk theatre, in the Ghent dialect.

The bronze man who sits by the entrance is Romain de Coninck, a man of the theatre who was close to the people, wrote pieces in the Ghent dialect and introduced this vivid idiom to television in a comic police series. His plays are still performed regularly. If this statue should disappear without trace during your visit then Romain is probably away being restored after being hit by a car. It wouldn't be the first time.

The theatre where drama flourished in the Ghent dialect

MUSEUM ARNOLD VANDER HAEGHEN ✪

This museum is probably the least well known by the inhabitants of Ghent, if they know it at all. Yet every year many Russian tourists come to the city simply to visit this museum. It so happens that Maurice Maeterlinck, winner of the Nobel Prize for Literature, is hugely popular in Russia and he is commemorated in this 18th-century former hotel through a display of his possessions and a reconstruction of his study. Those who are not keen on Maeterlinck can gaze at the tawdry Chinese salon with its silk wallpaper.

🔢 30B3
✉️ Veldstraat 82
☎️ 09–2257937
🕐 Tue–Sun 9:30–5
🍴 Patisserie Bloch in Veldstraat (£)
🚌 Tram 12, 41
♿ Good
💶 Cheap
↔️ Ketelvest (➤ 42)

MUSEUM VOOR SCHONE KUNSTEN ✪✪✪

Old and new stare each other in the face: the Museum of Fine Art is directly opposite the City Museum of Contemporary Art (S.M.A.K. ➤ 25), which is ideal for anyone who wants to spend the day among first-class works of art. The building is darker and gloomier than S.M.A.K.'s, but as far as the collection is concerned the museums are well matched. The oldest works are by Hiëronymous Bosch and the chronology progresses via Rubens, Brueghel the Younger, Frans Hals and an immensely moving canvas by Géricault. You arrive at the 20th century with Kokoschka and an important collection of etchings by the Ostend artist James Ensor (➤ 90).

🔢 30B1
✉️ Nicolaas De Liemaeckerplein 3
☎️ 09–2221703
🕐 Tue–Sun 9:30–5
🍴 Foyer S.M.A.K. (£)
🚌 Tram 12, 13; bus 5, 50
♿ Very good 💶 Moderate
↔️ S.M.A.K. (➤ 25)

Above: *art is also a Belgian export*

53

Food and Drink

Each inhabitant of Ghent drinks an average of 114 litres of beer a year, understandable when there is so much choice. Ghent is no place for teetotallers but those who like food will enjoy their stay.

Chips, subject of many Belgian jokes

Waterzooi

Although nearly all tourists are told that *waterzooi* is the local dish par excellence you will seldom smell the aroma of this nourishing dish in a Ghent house. Because the Leie became so polluted, the fish in this souplike stew was replaced by chicken. Furthermore, since a Ghent smelter caused a dioxin scandal in the country and people began to suspect the quality of the chicken, they have called the dish *rotzooi* (garbage) rather than *waterzooi* (casserole). Chicken is gradually regaining consumers' confidence but most restaurants still make their casserole with (imported) fish.

Tierenteyn mustard

Dijon mustard has a formidable rival in Tierenteyn mustard from Ghent. There are some people who pull a face if their ham has been dunked in a pot of Tierenteyn mustard, it makes others sneeze, but people who like strong flavours swear by this blend of Canadian, Ethiopian and Indian mustard seeds. What makes this different from other mustards is that the skins of the mustard seeds are not removed before the mustard is prepared. The Egyptians used mustard as an aphrodisiac, which is a nice bonus for some. You can find Ferdinand Tierenteyn's shop in the Groentenmarkt.

There are still visible traces of French-speaking Ghent

Kwak beer

Not for softies. The bottom of a Kwak glass is rounded so that there comes a point when all the beer rushes (*kwakt* in Dutch) into your mouth. The beer is actually named after the coachman Pauwel Kwak who designed the wooden frame that supports the glass. That meant that while he was working he did not need to keep hold of his glass the whole time. Because glasses like that are quite expensive, in the café Dulle Griet you will be asked to give up a shoe as a deposit. The shoe is then hung on the ceiling until your glass is returned empty and in one piece. Remember to wear clean socks when you have an evening out; your fellow drinkers will be eternally grateful. (Dulle Griet, Vrijdagmarkt ► 26, 36).

Coffee

It is a misunderstanding that needs to be corrected that coffee is particularly popular in southern Europe. On the contrary, the Swedes drink a massive 12kg per person per year, while the Italians are nowhere near a place on the podium. Antwerp is the world's most important coffee port and there are 140 coffee factories in the country. Belgium is a world leader in coffee preparation and for that reason alone you can drink Belgian coffee with confidence. The most fragrant address in Ghent is probably that of Mokabon, where the Mysore and Margogyp coffees await the connoisseur. (Mokabon, Donkersteeg).

In Belgium beer is sold in glasses and bottles of all shapes and sizes

Emperor Charles V even has a brand of gin named after him

Hommage aan de vaas

🕀 30B3
✉ Jan Breydelstraat 5
☎ 09-2256676
🕐 Tue-Sun 9:30-5
🍴 Excellent restaurants in the street (££)
🚊 Tram 1, 10, 11, 13
♿ Few
💷 Cheap
🔄 Gravensteen (▶ 18)

Above: design is looking for beauty in everyday objects

🕀 30B3
✉ Onderbergen 1
☎ 09-2250180
🕐 Sat-Sun 10–12AM
🍴 Pannenkoekenhuizen Onderbergen (£)
♿ Reasonable
💷 Moderate
🔄 Museum Arnold Vander Haeghen (▶ 53)
❓ Groups by arrangement

MUSEUM VOOR SIERKUNSTEN

You get a very strange feeling walking round this 18th-century aristocrats house. On the one hand you are walking through dusty and musty old rooms, and on the other hand there is a fresh modern part to discover. But the museum does have the desired effect. The old rooms belong to the De Coninck hotel that was once housed here and they show interiors from the 15th to the 19th centuries. The modern part provides space for temporary exhibitions, illustrating a particular aspect of design, a particular country or period. In the old section the emphasis is on form, in the new it is on design. It is a question of reflecting the spirit of the age.

PAND ✪✪✪

This 13th-century Dominican house is undoubtedly among the best preserved and most beautiful buildings in the city, even though it has suffered as a result of religious disputes, for example at the hands of the iconoclasts and in the time of Napoleon. In 1566 the contents of the library, including beautiful manuscripts, was thrown into the water. We know from the chronicles of Marcus van Vaernewijck that it had contained a great many books. According to him it was possible to walk right across the river on these books without getting wet feet. The friars had to rent out part of their 73m-long building as a warehouse because of financial problems. Since 1963 the house has belonged to the University of Ghent and it is used for conferences. Temporary exhibitions and a small museum of stained glass mean that the building is open to the public at weekends.

PATERSHOL (▶ 21, TOP TEN)

OPENBARE URINOIRS (PUBLIC URINALS)

Anyone who walks about the city will come across these brightly coloured urinals. They are actually squat concrete blocks; the decoration only appeared when the city was overrun by a wave of amateur graffiti 'artists'. Youngsters who are caught with a spray-can are often unable to pay the huge fines involved and so the task of repainting public toilets was thought up as an alternative punishment. Local people reacted so enthusiastically to the initiative that professional artists were soon also commissioned to paint the exterior of the urinals. Alas these artistic loos are men-only.

✉ Here and there in the city

DID YOU KNOW?

Don't be shocked if you see a gilded heap of dog mess with a cocktail flag sticking out of it. This is how an action committee campaigns against the thoughtlessness of dog owners.

OUDE POSTGEBOUW

The striking building in the Korenmarkt was the neo-gothic post office building until 1999. Local residents were keen to preserve it and backed a proposal to convert the post office into a shopping centre. The name 'Old Post Office' is used here for the first time. The architect Louis Cloquet who also designed the St Pietersstation and other buildings in the city, included in the facade portraits of the city fathers, Florence Nightingale and other important figures. No one knows the identity of the pretty girls and it is assumed that they were the architect's mistresses. The building was completed in 1910 and was one of the showpieces of the Ghent World Fair in 1913.

🚹 30B3
✉ Korenmarkt
🍴 Eetgelegenheden Korenmarkt (££)
🚃 Tram 12, 41
🔄 St Niklaaskerk (► 61)

The clock showed it was ten to eleven when the old post office gave way to a shopping centre

🔲 30A4
✉ Rabotstraat
🚊 Tram 13;
  bus 52, 53, 54, 69
↔ Prinsenhof (▶ 22)
🛥 Bootjes van Ghent/
  Benelux (▶ 20)

PRINSENHOF (▶ 22, TOP TEN)

RABOT ✪✪✪

Only two small sections remain standing of the 14km city walls that Ghent once had. One of them is the Rabot, a fortified sluice. Most visitors get to see this showpiece at the end of a boat trip. When the locks under the towers were opened it was possible to flood 15sq km of the surrounding land: an ideal strategy for slowing the advance of the enemy. Forty thousand Austrians discovered that the strategy worked.

The Rabot lost its military function a long time ago and it has since been an inn, a warehouse, electricity sub-station, nesting and breeding site for doves – the list could go on. These days the building can be hired by anyone who wants to entertain lavishly in an unusual location.

Solid and substantial:
the Rabot

SIKKEL ✪✪✪

This building on the corner between Hoogpoort, Biezekapelstraat and Nederpolder is a gem of a 14th-century aristocrat's house that takes its name from the family that built it: van der Zickelen. The complex is divided into three buildings: the large Sikkel, small Sikkel and rear Sikkel. The whole of it will certainly fire your imagination, and in addition Biezelkapelstraat is a very romantic little lane. It is one of the most peaceful corners of the city and because nowadays it houses the Academy of Music you can sometimes hear the voice of a would-be opera diva wafting out of the windows.

🔲 Not on the map
✉ Biezekapelstraat
🕐 During performances
🍴 Restaurants
  St Baafsplein (£)
🚊 Tram 40, 41, 42
↔ The Ghent Altarpiece
  (▶ 16)

DID YOU KNOW?

The famous Austrian court and ball culture is really a product of Ghent and was exported by Maximilian of Austria. He married Maria of Burgundy in the Prinsenhof, Ghent on 19 August 1477, at 6 o'clock in the morning.

A Walk Along the Scheldt

This is a very long, peaceful walk with hardly any historic monuments but it is a perfect introduction to the green belt in and around Merelbeke (▶ 86).

Leave the St Baafsabdij on the left and follow the river downstream along the Koepoortkaai. Five hundred metres further on you take the narrow path by the river, the Jongenstragel. At the end of the path cross the river but continue to follow along the tow-path, called Achtervisserij.

On your right stands the lovely little church of the Nieuwen Bosch Abbey and the cottages of the Onze-Lieve-Vrouw Ter Hove (▶ 13, 52). On the left hand side there are the buildings of the newspaper *Het Volk*, a number of alleys and architectural gems of gentlemens houses.

Take the busy Brusselspoortstraat under the Keizerviaduct and turn right immediately, on to Pynaertkaai.

You need only carry straight on. There is a footpath that runs for kilometres alongside the Scheldt. The tow-path, at one point known as *Meierij*, takes you past workers' neighbourhoods and finally out to the Ringvaart, the canal that had to save the port of Ghent from obsolescence after World War II.

Just before you reach the yacht harbour and the lock gate of the Ringvaart you will see the Liedermeerspark and you can connect with the excursions in Merelbeke.

Distance
7km

Time
2.5–4 hours

Start point
Julius Devigneplein
⊞ 31A3

End point
Liedermeerspark (Merelbeke)
⊞ Not on the map

Lunch
Take a picnic

Time for a quiet walk along the Leie

🕂 31A3
✉ Gandastraat 7
☎ 09–2251585
🕐 Apr–Oct: Tue–Sun 9:30–5
🚌 Bus 38
♿ Reasonable
🖐 Moderate

ST BAAFSABDIJ ✪✪✪

The oldest building in the city (founded in 630 by St Amand, a French missionary), St Bavo's Abbey was on a site at the last bend of the River Leie before it joins the Scheldt. The Celtic word for confluence is *ganda* from which you can recognise the origin of the city's name (▶ 10). The abbey became a place of pilgrimage but is not much more than a ruin these days and for that Emperor Charles V was responsible. He had the abbey demolished in order to build a barracks for Spanish mercenaries on the site. But with a little effort you can imagine yourself in the medieval dormitory or the abbots' communal lavatory. The Romanesque wall paintings and parts of the cloisters are relatively well preserved. The collection of stone carvings, the huge refectory and the central cloister garden will certainly appeal to visitors.

This abbey has its place in English History too. Edward III, King of England, stayed here during the Hundred Years War and his son, John of Gaunt (Gaunt being an English version of Ghent, ▶ 14), was born here.

Visitors on a conducted tour of the oldest building in the city, St Baafsabdij

ST BAAFSKATHEDRAAL (▶ 23, TOP TEN)
ST ELISABETHBEGIJNHOF (▶ 24, TOP TEN)

ST JORISHOF ✪✪

This hotel is the oldest in Europe; under French rule it was called Cour St Georges. It was the home of the crossbow archers' guild, the 'VIP tent' during the festival of the Chambers of Rhetoric (literary/debating societies) in 1439, and in its time has received dozens of prominent figures from the political and artistic worlds. Many patronise the restaurant because of the historic banquets held there, and because of the manageress who set a new Belgian record when she won the national marathon.

✚ 30B3
✉ Botermarkt 2
☎ 09–2242424
🍴 Restaurant in the hotel (££)
🚋 Tram 21, 22, 40, 41, 42; bus 3, 16, 17, 18, 19, 38
↔ Stadhuis (▶ 66)

Above: *Europe's oldest hotel still keeps up with the times*

ST NIKLAASKERK ✪✪✪

Each guild had its own patron saint and church. St Niklaaskerk was the sailors' church and many people think it is the most beautiful of all the 59 churches in the city. Building work began in 1200, the heyday of the Scheldt Gothic style. From the tower you have a wonderful view of the building which is lit up with green light at night. It is amazing to see so much light in the church building itself because this is unusual in the Low Countries. At the beginning of 1900 little shops were built against the church walls but they were demolished because of the 1913 Ghent World Fair. You can still find traces of them in Klein Turkje street. There have been discussions about whether to re-create the picturesque little buildings in the street scene or leave it as it stands.

✚ 30B3
✉ Korenmarkt, Klein Turkije, E: Braunplein
🕐 Daily 2–5:30
🍴 Restaurants on Korenmarkt (££)
🚋 Tram 12, 41; bus 3, 16, 17, 18, 19, 38
♿ Good
📷 Free
↔ Metsershuis (▶ 51)
❓ Some parts are undergoing restoration

In the Know

If you only have a short time to visit Ghent and would like to get a real flavour of the city, here are some ideas:

10
Ways to be a Local

- As soon as a problem arises, demand a **people's referendum**.
- You hate the **parking problems** and the highly illogical road signs.
- Your watch just happens to stop in the **pub**.
- You **laugh** when that happens.
- You always laugh at the **tunes on mobile telephones**.
- If you can **act like an artist** you are most probably an artist.
- In the winter you miss the **Ghent Festivals**.
- In the summer you **moan about the crowds**.
- You think it's a scandal that as a taxpayer you have to pay for **S.M.A.K.** modern art museum.
- You don't like **drunks** unless you are drunk yourself.

10
Good Places to have Lunch

Artevelde (££)
✉ Vrijdagmarkt 6
☎ 09–2335288 . Flemish specialities such as *waterzooi*, stew and hotpot.

Avalon (£)
✉ Geldmunt 32
☎ 09–2243724. All organic food. Lunch 12–2

De Grill (££)
✉ Korenlei 23 ☎ 09–22 50974. Fish and meat grills, speciality *cote à l'os*.

Het spijker (££)
✉ Graslei 10 ☎ 09–23 40635. *Waterzooi* in an historic setting.

De Foyer Theatercafé (££)
✉ St Baafsplein 17
☎ 09–2253275. Simple sandwiches and sophisticated cuisine.

Belfort (££)
✉ Magheleinstraat
☎ 09–2241291. Pizzeria but also has French cuisine.

Bloch (£)
✉ Veldstraat 62
☎ 09–2257085. First rate Jewish pâtisserie.

Brooderie (£)
✉ Jan Breydelstraat 8
☎ 09–2250623. Small sandwiches with all kinds of smoked delicacies.

Foyer S.M.A.K. (£)
✉ Citadelpark
☎ 09–2211703. Tasty and healthy cuisine in an arty atmosphere.

Krokantino (£)
✉ Korte Munt 8
☎ 09–2242729. Various snacks.

Bloch: regular haunt of those with a sweet tooth

10

Photogenic Streets

- Ballenstraat
- Bennesteeg
- Biezekapelstraat
- Corduwanierstraat
- Donkersteeg
- Graslei
- Jan Breydelstraat
- Provenierstraat
- Serpentstraat
- Vanderdonckdoorgang

5

Essential Things To Do

- Listen to a Carillon concert from the Belfort (➤ 115).
- Visit the S.M.A.K. (➤ 25).

Left: street theatre is one of the sights in fine weather

- Take a boat trip on the river or canal (➤ 20).
- Eat some chocolate.
- Go out on a Thursday evening (➤ 113).

Catholic Flanders for sale

5

Best Views

- St Michielsbrug
- Donjon Gravensteen
- Kathedraaltoren
- Skipiste Blaarmeersen
- University Hospital Restaurant

30B3
St Michielshelling
Restaurants in the area (££)
Tram 12, 41;
bus 3, 16, 17, 18, 19, 38
Good
Kuip van Gent (➤ 20)

Above: *coming over the St Michielsbrug is still the best way to enter the city*

30B3
St Michielshelling
During the Eucharist
Restaurants on
St Michielsbrug (££)
Tram 12, 41;
bus 3, 16, 17, 18, 19, 38
Very good Free
St Michielsbrug (➤ 64)

ST MICHIELSBRUG ✪✪✪

Low swing-bridges slowed down traffic both on land and on water and the construction of the St Michielsbrug in 1910 did away with the congestion on the route to Bruges. It is the only large bridge in the city centre and Japanese tourists who have only a short time to see the city are brought here by their tour guide to get a quick impression of the city. It is a platform from which you can admire the guild houses on the Graslei and Korenlei, the three towers, the St Michielskerk and the Pand. This is picture-postcard Ghent, the perspective from which you can view the historic core of the city with a minimum of passing traffic to distract you.

ST MICHIELSKERK ✪✪✪

If you are not going to attend the celebration of the Eucharist in St Michael's Church you need read no further. The church is closed except for the liturgy in an attempt to keep the treasures, including *Christ on the Cross* by Antoon van Dyck, out of the hands of evil-intentioned visitors. The parish seems to have learned its lesson from the iconoclasm of 1566 and does not want to have to pick up the pieces again.

St Michael is the patron saint of the brewers. Medieval brewers each sold about 400 litres of beer per head of population annually so the coffers of their guild were well filled. The brewers wanted to use their pennies to build the largest church in Belgium in a symbolic gesture against the other guilds. They wanted to crown their church with a soaring 130m high tower. The mere 24m stump that you see today demonstrates that they had seriously underestimated the cost of the project. The Cathedral of Our Lady in Antwerp remains the largest church in Belgium.

ST PIETERSABDIJ ✪✪

There was already an abbey on this site in 630 and it was to become the richest in the district. But in the turbulent Flanders of the 16th century the iconoclasts destroyed the building completely. A century later, as the spirit of the Counter Reformation blew through the Arteveldestad, St Pietersabdij rose again, larger and more impressive than before. That is until the country fell into French hands because then the clergy were chased out of the abbey and the building became a military barracks. The actual church building has best survived the damage and, as well as the memorial to Isabella of Austria, it contains a number of other treasures. Important exhibitions are held here regularly, you can visit the school museum and the abbey contains the Centrum voor Kunst en Cultuur (Centre for Art and Culture).

🔲 30B2
✉ St Pietersplein 14
☎ 09-2228050
🕐 Mon–Thu, Sat 9–12:15 and 1:30–5:15. Closed on feast days
🍴 Mosselhuis on St Pietersplein (££)
🚌 Bus 5, 50
♿ Good
💰 Moderate
🔄 Boekentoren (▶ 34)

A colossal abbey, ostentatious symbol of the Counter Reformation

ST VEERLEPLEIN ✪✪

This small square was not always just somewhere to eat an ice cream in peace, to look at the Gravensteen from a pavement café or watch the trams come and go. The middle of the square where a lion now stands enthroned on his plinth was the site of the stake during the reign of the fanatical Philip II. It was the time of the edicts of the Inquisition and crazy witch hunts. Mind you, women in Ghent did not need to be burned at the stake. A woman was regarded as a lesser creature so it was a sin to waste firewood on her: she was drowned or beheaded. It is quite likely that many men who were condemned to death regretted that they belonged to the superior sex.

🔲 30B3/4
🍴 A few restaurants in the area (££)
🚋 Tram 1, 10, 11, 13
♿ Very good
🔄 Gravensteen (▶ 18)

SPIJKER ✪✪✪

This is the oldest house on the River Leie. It was built in 1200 and is a typical example of Romanesque bourgeois architecture. *Spijkeren* means to store goods and this was the place where grain was kept until it was offered for sale on the Korenmarkt (➤ 46). The Calvinists had their university here until they fled, driven out by fanatical Catholics. The building served as a student house until well into the 20th century. Nowadays beers are tapped competently here and the level of the pub itself is an indication of how much lower the streets were in the Middle Ages.

✚ 30B3
✉ Graslei 10
☎ 09–2340635
🍴 Reasonable restaurant in the area (££)
🚌 Tram 12, 41; bus 3, 16, 17, 18, 19, 38, 3
♿ Moderate
↔ Tolhuisje (➤ 67)

The Stadhuis is a hotch-potch of building styles

STADHUIS ✪✪✪

Emperor Charles V suffered seriously from megalomania and wanted to build the largest city hall in the world in the city of his birth. It had to surpass all its high Gothic predecessors and be elevated and proud. It did not turn out like that, however. His wars drained the exchequer and there was no money for the city hall. Nevertheless the Stadhuis is interesting architecturally. It illustrates perfectly the building trends through the ages; half has a Gothic facade, the other half was influenced by the spirit of the Renaissance and was constructed in the classical style.

✚ 30B3
✉ Botermarkt 1
☎ 09–2665221
⏱ Only in the summer months in the afternoon
🍴 Hungarian restaurant in Hoogpoort (££)
🚌 Bus 3, 16, 17, 18, 19, 38
♿ Few
🎫 Free
↔ St Jorishof (➤ 61)
❓ Group visits only by arrangement

STEDELIJK MUSEUM VOOR AKTUELE KUNST (S.M.A.K.) (➤ 25, TOP TEN)

TOLHUISJE ⭐⭐

Although it would be difficult to find a smaller house in the city Tolhuisje is not actually the smallest. This little house, now a tavern, was actually built in 1700 in a small alley that was intended to make the Leie easier to reach as a source of water in case of fire. A similar fire alley is still visible and connects the Graslei with the nearby Korenmarkt (▶ 46). This is where the skippers had to pay their tolls. Interestingly, every year the management of the toll house was changed to guard against the chance of corruption and favouritism making their way into the system.

✚	30B3
✉	Graslei 11
☎	09–2243090
🍴	Café in the area (£)
🚃	Tram 12, 41; bus 3, 16, 17, 18, 19, 38
♿	Good
↔	Kuip van Gent (▶ 20)

Left: *in the past the money went to the toll officials, now it goes to the pub landlady*

Below: *exotic wares follow the strong immigrant population*

TURKISHTOWN ⭐

No, this is not New York, where some nationalities have their own city within a city, but by analogy the Turkish community in Ghent has given the name 'Turkishtown' to their area. This is in the neighbourhood of Sleepstraat where many ethnic minorities run restaurants, manage a *hammam* (Turkish bath) or run a carpet shop. Yet not everyone uses the name Turkishtown because it would encourage the ghetto mentality and hinder integration in the city. Besides, the Belgian individuals who live in Sleepstraat are not disregarded. But anyone who wants to have a Turkish kebab, or buy apple tobacco for his *narghile*, or peppermint tea, knows where to find them.

✚	31A4
✉	Sleepstraat and surrounding area
🍴	Turkish restaurants (£)
🚃	Tram 40, 42
♿	Very good

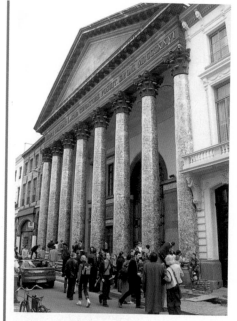

When Jan Fabre covered the pillars of the university with ham there was a national scale witch-hunt

🕂 30B3
✉ Volderstraat 9
🎫 Only during events
🍴 A few snack bars in the area (£)
🚊 Tram 12, 13
♿ Few
↔ Veldstraat (► 69)

UNIVERSITY (UNIVERSITEIT) ★★

The University of Ghent has moved all over the place in the course of its history and even now the various faculties are scattered about the city and some are still on the move. The senate house in Volderstraat dates from 1816, when the teaching was still in Latin. If you have the opportunity do visit the staircase and the semi-circular senate hall; it is highly decorated, a proud monument to neo-classicism. The university reached its heyday in the 1930s when the Ghent students were taught for the first time in their mother tongue, Dutch. In the year 2000 this building hit the headlines when the artist Jan Fabre covered it with ham.

🕂 30B1
✉ Overpoortstraat
↔ S.M.A.K. (► 25)
❓ The later in the evening the more the atmosphere hots up

UNIVERSITY DISTRICT (UNIVERSITEITSBUURT) ★

In spite of the fact that the various faculties are spread out here and there in the city, Ghent does have a street where all the university students meet up: Overpoortstraat. It is tremendously busy here, especially on Thursday evenings during the academic year, and you will be struck by the bacchanalian intensity of the student life. This area has the highest number of pubs and the police often have to divert the traffic because it is impossible to drive through the crowds of people. Parents who happen to see this street on a Thursday evening might begin to have serious worries about their children's studies.

VAN RYHOVESTEEN ✪✪

François van Ryhove was a formidable fighter against idolatry and in 1577 he founded a Calvinist republic in Ghent. The Catholic leaders were thrown behind bars in the cellar of this building, where the archaeological service is now housed. You can see the recent discoveries in the covered walkway. Here they are cleaned up and their historical value assessed. The courtyard garden is a peaceful oasis but until a few years ago it was even more attractive because it contained sculptures.

🕂 30B3
✉ Onderstraat 22
🕐 The courtyard: daily 9–5
🍴 Cafés and restaurants on the Vrijdagmarkt (£)
🚌 Bus 3, 16, 17, 18, 19, 38
♿ Reasonable
🎟 Free
↔ Vrijdagmarkt (➤ 26)

VELDSTRAAT ✪

This long street is the most important one for shopping and all the large chains do their best to make it look exactly like any other western shopping street. On Saturdays you can almost walk on the heads of the crowds. At the junction with Volderstraat, however, you can find several shops that look just as they did a hundred years ago: the exquisite cigar and fountain-pen shop Caron, the celebrated pâtisserie Bloch and the (in the main French-speaking) bookshop Herkenrath which has often been visited in the past by prominent writers. These are also the only shops with people living above them. At the rear of Veldstraat, along the Leie, there are a number of Chinese tea houses that, at the time of the *belle époque*, were frequented by ladies dressed up to go shopping.

🕂 30B3
✉ Veldstraat
🍴 Snack bars and pubs in the street (£)
🚃 Tram 12, 41
♿ Very good
↔ Museum Arnold Vander Haeghen (➤ 53)

Shopping, browsing and strolling in Veldstraat

69

WHAT TO SEE

30B3
Tussen St Veerleplein and Vleeshuistragel
Tram 1, 10, 11, 13, 40, 42

On Sundays many local people canoe through the city

VISHALLEN ⭐⭐

This once bustling historic building is now in danger of being lost forever because it is standing empty. The fish market has lost its purpose since no fish have been taken out of the River Leie, let alone sold, for more than a century due to the poor, polluted, quality of the water. In 1998 the building was the subject of a fierce argument. A plan to replace it with a modern glass construction was forwarded, but this was opposed on the grounds that it would have looked out of place beside the old architecture. Half the city took to the streets, demanded a referendum and again that well-known Ghent stubbornness came to the fore. The glass construction was put on ice, and the old fish market is still standing, awaiting its destiny. The best-preserved section is the huge entrance on the St Veerleplein, where there is a sculpture representing the confluence of the Leie and the Scheldt.

Not on the map
Vleeshuistragel, Pensmarkt and Groentenmarkt
Only during events
Pubs on the Groentenmarkt (£)
Tram 1, 10, 11, 12, 13, 40, 41, 42
Good
Depends on events
Gravensteen (►18)

VLEESHUIS ⭐⭐

In 15th-century Ghent certain butchers were banned and all meat had to be sold in the covered meat market in order to make the control of price and quality easier. You can still see by the facade along the Leie that meat used to be brought in by boat. The small lean-to buildings on Groentenmarkt were used for processing offal which was made into puddings that the poor could afford. Some of these buildings now house small shops or cafés. The wooden trusses are worth looking at, but alas the Vleeshuis has been waiting for a new use for a long time.

For years there has been talk of making the Vleeshuis a covered market as it used to be but that idea has been shelved for the time being. Now and then an exhibition or a medieval breakfast bring this historic building to life once more.

VOORUIT ✪✪✪

Vooruit is called 'the bastion of socialism' and between the two world wars it certainly was. Later this art nouveau palace was abandoned to its fate in a pathetic condition. At one point it was close to being demolished until, in 1982, a group of young people joined forces and turned this glorious former meeting place into a true cultural centre. It was not long before Vooruit became a concept in the world of the performing arts.

All the big rock bands, theatre companies and authors tread the boards in the Vooruit cultural centre, and glittering parties take place in the ballroom. The foyer – in spite of having the appearance of a bleak refectory – is a pleasant place to meet.

✚ 30B2
✉ St Pietersnieuwstraat 23
☎ 09-2255643
🕐 15 Aug–15 Jul: daily to 3
🍴 Food and drink in the building (£)
🚌 Bus 5, 6, 50
♿ Good
↔ Licht (► 48)

VRIJDAGMARKT
(► 26, TOP TEN)

KARELKE WAERI ✪
(STATUE)

Karelke Waeri was a Ghent folk singer whose heart was with the people. The lyrics to his songs were biting, poetic, ambiguous and written in the Flemish vernacular. This 'totem pole' by Walter de Buck illustrates snatches of songs from Waeri's work, for example, the firemen from the song of that name. Waeri wrote this number after the fire brigade had turned out but had left their water tank behind by mistake. The fire was put out anyway – by connecting the hoses to the cesspit. Walter de Buck recorded a CD with Waeri songs on it in order to pay for the sculpture.

In a final ironic twist, the Dutch-speaking Flemish Waeri was murdered by a French-speaker and his widow then remarried a Walloon.

✚ Not on the map
✉ Bij St Jacobs
🍴 Pubs and restaurants on Vrijdagmarkt (££)
🚌 Bus 3, 16, 17, 18, 19, 38, 55, 57, 58, 69
↔ Vrijdagmarkt (► 26)

The characters from the works of the folk singer Karelke Waeri

30A2
Watersportlaan
Sport and Recreation
Office 09–2218071
Bus 6
Very good

*The water-sports arena,
a meeting place for
sports enthusiasts*

WATER-SPORTS ARENA

Ghent has a thing about rowing. In 1909 to everyone's amazement the crew from Ghent was victorious at the prestigious Henley Regatta in England. In 1955 Ghent organised the European championships and saw the Soviet Union in particular take the medals. The rowing lanes at the water-sports arena (watersportbaan) are now among the most hated in the world because records are no longer broken there: the water is not deep enough, which means that rowers have to use double the muscle power to counteract the drag of the water.

Apart from oarsmen, the water-sports arena is full of fishing lines and half the sport lovers in Ghent come here to jog. A circuit measures exactly 5km; it is easy to work out how far you have driven yourself, and if you are a distance runner you can run on a Finnish track (made of bark chippings). The sculpture *Verheerlijking van de Sport* (Glorification of Sport) and the Higher Institute for Physical Education fit in here very well.

Campers should take their water sports equipment with them since they look out on to the water-sports arena from their tents.

A Walk to the Ruins of St Baafsabdij

A peaceful walk away from the city centre and a simple one to follow too.

Go to the level of the huge building of Bond Moyson in Waaistraat and walk straight on.

In the 19th century, this neighbourhood was built up by rich industrialists who speculated that the area of the Vrijdagmarkt (► 26) would become a large shopping centre. To their great disappointment this honour fell to Veldstraat (► 69).

Via Speldenstraat and Goudstraat you come out at Minnemeers.

The Museum of Industrial Architecture and Textiles here is worth visiting, as well as NT2, an annexe to the Dutch Theatre Company of Ghent. The Huidvettersbrug is one of the prettiest bridges in Ghent and could well be linking two areas of Paris. The literary quarter is on the opposite bank of the Leie. The lock on the Baudelookaai marks the end of the Ghent Basin (► 20) and is only opened by arrangement with the lock keeper.

The junction with Steendam can be busy. Continue to follow the Leie and walk along Nieuwbrugkaai.

The branch of the Leie on your left provides a direct link to the modern port area. The narrow streets on the opposite side are built on the historic site of the abbey and a Spanish castle. Art lovers can visit the large gallery on the right-hand side.

After the Veerkaai you come out on the Vigneplein. To your right, on the corner, stands the Van Eyck swimming pool that still looks as it did in 1920 and which is regularly used for filming. You will see that the Leie divides into two here and comes to an end.

Ghent was founded on this spot in 630 (► 10, 60) and on the opposite side lie the ruins of the first buildings of this settlement.

Distance
4km

Time
2–5 hours

Start point
Vrijdagmarkt
➕ 31A3

End point
Vigneplein
➕ 31A3

Lunch
Restaurants on
Vrijdagmarkt (££)

The Huidevettersbrug connects the city with a neighbourhood where it is no accident that many writers have taken up residence

30B4
Kraanlei 79
09–2240041
Restaurants Oudburg (££)
Tram 40, 42
Good
Kinderen Alynshospitaal
(➤ 43)

Giving drink to the thirsty is probably the most attractive work of mercy

WERKEN VAN BARMHARTIGHEID

The house where the flamboyant Mrs Temmerman sold her typical Ghent sweets has a unique 17th-century gable on which the seven works of mercy are depicted. Anyone who has had to learn them by heart will probably still recognise them. It will perhaps take longer to find the work of mercy 'Burying the dead' and the passer-by can count only six. Look for the solution on the roof which is surmounted by an urn. The house stands companionably next to another attractive gable, *De Fluitspeler* (Flute Player) which displays an allegory of the five senses depicted in terracotta. Looking at a house like this can sometimes reveal interesting puzzles.

WERREGARENSTRAATJE

Graffiti are absolutely forbidden and have cost the city a small fortune in restoration. Obviously for some the urge to use the spray-can is stronger than the law and, alas, buildings have to be cleaned regularly. Because the graffiti artists should not give expression to their creative urges on historic buildings, and also to show *some* appreciation of this form of art, the city gave them a street where graffiti are tolerated. The narrow street is known as 'graffiti street'. Anyone who can stand the stench of urine can look into the garden of the Van Ryhovesteen (➤ 69) from this street.

30B3
Werregarenstraat
Good pubs in Hoogpoort (£)
Tram 21, 22, 40, 41, 42; bus 3, 16, 17, 18, 19, 38
Very good
Stadhuis (➤ 66)

WESTERBEGRAAFPLAATS ✪✪

The ideological opposite of the Catholic cemetery Campo Santo (▶ 19) is the Westerbegraafplaats near the Ghent–Bruges Canal. This became the last resting place for the freethinkers and unbelievers and earned the nickname 'beggars' graveyard'. It was not until the middle of the 20th century that the authorities gave permission for the consecration of several graves. Of the many famous people buried here the most notable ones are writers: Cyriel Buysse, Virginie Loveling, Johan Disse and the composer of the Flemish national anthem, Karel Miry.

➕ Not on the map
✉ Palinghuizen 143
🕐 Daily 9–6
🚋 Tram 1, 10, 11
♿ Very good

The brothel closed its doors centuries ago but couples still meet here

ZWAENE ✪

Swans have always been a symbol of beer – and girls. Up to and including the 17th century this building was a pub and a harbour brothel. Rumour has it that Emperor Charles V used to come here incognito to have a good time. The building is now in a sorry state. It has been empty for years and although certain politicians have bemoaned the fact, the slow deterioration continues. As often happens in this city, investors are put off by the high prices of historic buildings and the strict regulations on restoration. For a while there has been a rumour that an American would like to open an hotel here.

➕ Not on the map
✉ Korenlei 9
🍴 Restaurants on Koren- and Graslei (££)
🚋 Tram 12, 41
🔄 Kuip van Ghent (▶ 20)

Exploring the Area

It is often said that Ghent is situated between Bruges and Antwerp not only geographically but that it is also intermediate in character: Bruges, with its museums and celebrated for its medieval pomp; Antwerp a port city and metropolis.

Ghent is a first-class centre from which to visit the rest of Belgium because it has good train services to the various Flemish towns. If you prefer to drive you will experience the luxury of driving on well-lit motorways during the evening and at night. Belgium is also the country most visible from the moon, to the great annoyance of environmental activists and astronomers. Ghent is surrounded by a green belt that is visible in good weather from the roof of St Baafskathedraal. The Leie meanders through an area of breathtaking natural beauty which was the base for many artists of the Latem School. The many castles and the picturesque villages along the Leie remind visitors of the Loire valley. You will long remember the colourful images of the flower nurseries.

> '*Ah, Ghent, bad Ghent.* '
>
> 15th-century chronicler at
> the Court of Brussels

———————•———————

Left: *the area around Ghent is really magnificent*

Accessibility
Aalst is 23km from Ghent and by car is best approached via the E40 towards Brussels. Between 5AM and 11PM two trains an hour leave St Pietersstation.

Aalst

This small carnival town on the banks of the Dender is often mistakenly overlooked as a tourist attraction. Nevertheless without a doubt Aalst has the most splendid medieval bell tower still completely intact and it contains the world's oldest carillon. The small market square with its bell tower and the arcaded Borse van Amsterdam market make a visit to this town well worthwhile.

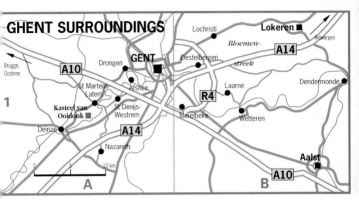

GHENT SURROUNDINGS

Lochristi · Lokeren ■ · Antwerpen · *Bloemen-* · A14 · GENT ■ · Destelbergen · *streek* · Drongen · Dendermonde ● · Afsnee · St Martens-Latem · Laarne · R4 · Brugge, Oostene · A10 · Kasteel van Ooidonk ■ · St Denijs-Westrem · Merelbeke · Wetteren · Deinze ● · A14 · Nazareth · Aalst ■ · 0 5 10 km · A · A10 · B

1

In Aalst, like many Flemish towns, there are printing works but what is unusual is that here Dirk Martens set up the first printing press in the Low Countries. The former hospital is now a museum where many old printing presses are on display.

The St Martinuskerk, the largest church in Belgium before it was damaged by fire, houses innumerable works of art (including a Rubens) and a golden line runs across the church. The sun strikes this line precisely at 12 noon.

The town has become better known since the filming of the book *Pieter Daens* by Louis Paul Boon (a local man) and people have made their way to the Daens Museum where the struggle of the workers for a better life is illustrated by means of displays of photographs and documents.

But above all Aalst is the carnival town. Every year before the beginning of Lent the town erupts in a great celebration that is not always appreciated by every outsider. To many visitors the local people seem to behave in a vulgar fashion and to be having too much fun at the expense of others.

There are plenty of other reasons for visiting this 19th-century industrial town. If you are a gourmet and have a sweet tooth go for the 'Aalst Flan'. Book-lovers see a visit as a pilgrimage in honour of the author Louis Paul Boon and, in the little village of Erembodegem, they can look for the Kapellekensbaan, the street which gave its name to his most famous book, *Little Chapel Road*.

Above left: *the Aalsterse Oud Hospitaal is a place you would want to put in your pocket and take home*

The Venice of the North, Amsterdam or Bruges?

Bruges

The public is so fond of Bruges (Brugge) that the city receives 95 percent of its income from tourism. It is indeed a wonderful place. Its nickname is 'Bruges the beautiful' and seeing Bruges before you leave Flanders is almost obligatory.

'Bruges the beautiful' on the one hand, 'Bruges the lifeless on the other'. And indeed, after the museums close the place becomes deathly quiet and there is hardly anything going on. So you may prefer to use Ghent as a base from which to visit Bruges, although many people do it the other way round.

It is the green and picturesque character of Bruges and the fact that it is free of many elements of contemporary life that draws people from thousands of kilometres away. The canals flow between the medieval buildings and past weeping willows, hence the title 'Venice of the North'. Beside the Minnewater (Lake of Love) – a name that in itself makes the heart beat faster – courting couples lie on the grass, while several hundred metres further on the sisters stroll through what is probably one of the most famous begijnhofs in the world, dating from the 13th century.

Together with the Uffizi Gallery in Florence, Bruges is a mecca for lovers of medieval art. Here you can admire the works of Old Masters such as Hugo van der Goes, Pieter Pourbus, Hans Memling, Jeroen Bosch, Rogier van der Weyden and many others in the Groeningemuseum, one of the top attractions in the city. Memling has his own small but outstanding museum, housed in the chapel of an ancient hospital, St Jans, which is also worth a visit.

A few drops of blood, brought back from the Crusades and said to have come from Jesus Christ, are kept in the Basiliek van het Heilig Bloed (Basilica of the Holy Blood), a 12th-century chapel.

If you like counting steps you can climb the bell tower and look out to the North Sea in peace and quiet – at least, as long as you keep an eye on the time because the 47 bells can sound very loud.

Breidelstraat is the place to buy lace, the product that for a long time guaranteed the sisters in the begijnhof their financial independence and still one of Bruges' proudest exports.

Anyone who has already taken a boat trip in Ghent will find the boats are more crowded in Bruges. But at least they are newer – the boats in Ghent have already been in service in Bruges but were regarded as too shabby.

In the Onze-Lieve-Vrouwekathedraal look for the impressive tombs of Charles the Bold and Mary of Burgundy. Nowadays, when a local inhabitant dies, his or her death notice is printed and displayed on the walls of this Brabant Gothic building.

Bruges is a picture-postcard place, a dream for film producers, but its authenticity is sometimes disputed. In 1998 the city had its pride dented when a Briton claimed that Bruges is almost entirely fake. The outrage this provoked is quite understandable because Bruges stands or falls by tourism. But imitation or authentic, dead or living, the fact remains that Bruges is 'the beautiful' and leaves an unforgettable impression on its visitors. The visitor who is beginning to feel like a local from Ghent had better beware. The inhabitants of Bruges built a Ghent Gate to keep out invaders from that city.

✉ St Pietersstation
🚆 Two trains an hour to Bruges
↔ Ostend

The tomb of Mary of Burgundy

✉ St Pietersstation
🚆 Two trains an hour to
Antwerp

Antwerp

Antwerp is buzzing. You feel that as soon as you leave Centraal Station and see the moving crowds of people. One in five Flemings lives in Antwerp. It is patently obvious that this is a big city and anyone who is only used to the pace of Ghent is in for a shock.

This city is a hive of activity where everything possible is done to keep its place in the top five ports of the world. To be quite honest, you would have to look a long way to find someone who was bored here.

Diamonds are a girl's best friend; women will find plenty of glitter in this diamond city. The Meir and Keyserlei together form a huge shopping boulevard, good for hours of pleasant and enjoyable shopping.

You can relax on Groenplaats while you drink a *bolleke* at a pavement café, the perfect setting for a spot of people watching, or why not visit the zoo where you can confirm that we are indeed descended from the apes.

For a helping of architecture go to the city hall, the largest building designed in the Renaissance style in the Low Countries. The cathedral is Belgium's largest church and has many works of art including a masterpiece by Rubens.

Cellar pubs, discos and folk cafés give you plenty of opportunity to become acquainted with Flemish conviviality, although if you want more peace and quiet you can potter round the antique shops in Kloosterstraat.

Like Aalst, Antwerp is proud of her past as a printing centre; bibliophiles will lose their hearts in the Plantin Moretus Museum, which houses some 20,000 books plus printing equipment and works of art.

Take a boat trip round the harbour, a visit to the oldest Romanesque fortress, the Steen, which since 1952 has housed the National Maritime Museum, or the Vleeshuis.

Don't worry: Antwerp will certainly keep you in its grasp.

You can take a boat trip from the harbour as far as the Dutch frontier

A Walk Through Antwerp

Begin at the imposing Centraal Station, designed by the Belgian architect Delacenserie (1904), proudly referred to by the locals as 'The Railway Cathedral'. As you leave you will see on your right Antwerp Zoo, one of the oldest and most famous zoos in the world, and on your left the diamond quarter.

Many gold and diamond shops are in fact built into the walls of the station. Anyone who is interested can visit the diamond museum, where for example on a Saturday afternoon you can see a diamond-cutter at work. The history of the diamond trade and the production of jewellery are revealed in the museum.

Distance
4–6km

Time
2–6 hours

Start point
Centraal Station

End point
The Steen

Lunch
Along the way you will find any number of places to eat to suit every budget

Take the wide avenue in front of you, Keyserlei, and cross over Teniersplaats. Continue via Leysstraat which runs into the shopping street, the Meir.

Both avenues emphasise the big-city character of Antwerp. Stroll through this pedestrian zone especially on a Saturday afternoon and do not miss the splendour of the facades.

Keep the cathedral on your right, cross over Handschoenmarkt and reach the Grote Markt via the Quinten Metsys well.

You need to buy a ticket for the zoo if you want to see a real elephant

You see the city hall right in front of you, flanked by the Brabo Fountain.

If you leave the Grote Markt, with the city hall on your right, and pass into the Suikkerui you get a view of the harbour, a port of international importance.

On Steenplein you can visit one of the oldest buildings in Antwerp: the Steen. This fortress dating from 1200 was originally a stone reinforcement of the walls, later it was used as a prison and nowadays it houses the National Maritime Museum. You will see a number of vessels out of the water which form part of the open-air museum.

83

✉ These villages are easy to reach via the Antwerp-sesteenweg and the Dendermondsesteenweeg

Flower District

What makes the villages to the east of Ghent special is that they are responsible for one of the trademarks of Ghent: floriculture. The fields here are carpets of colour and just when you decide you want a change you catch sight of a castle, as if it were perfectly normal to have so many huge buildings concentrated in one area.

This area east of Ghent begins after the train station of Damport and the best way to immerse yourself in the wealth of flowers and castles is to hire a bicycle and simply take off. No problems about finding your way, there are plenty of signposts to get you to your destination without any headaches, and back to Ghent in good time.

In the spring azaleas are a feast for the eyes. They are particularly common in St Amandsberg, Oostakker, Lochristi (the main centre) and Destelbergen. These villages are easy to reach via Antwerpsesteenweg and Dendermonsesteenweg and are only a few kilometres from Ghent itself. In addition Destelbergen has a magnificent castle route marked on the road that leads through rustic hamlets, avenues and parks.

If you are fond of begonias you need to be out and about between July and September to see your favourites in bloom, and anyone whose mouth waters at the word 'strawberries' should without a doubt visit the village of Beervelde in May or June, when these little red treats are being picked and sold.

River Leie at Drongen

When the sun shines many families from Ghent take a trip out to Drongen. They walk along the Leie, eat pancakes or drink a strong local beer and dream that they are rich enough to buy a house by the romantic River Leie where property is becoming more and more expensive.

The rustic village of Drongen is about ten minutes ride from Ghent and found on the banks of the Leie which looks rather different here compared to its course through Ghent. It is almost impossible to imagine that you are only 3km from St Baafskathedraal and that the surroundings are so rural.

One noticeable feature is a retirement home for priests. The building has kept its original atmosphere; there has been a Premonstratensian abbey here since the 12th century. The Premonstratensians, sometimes called Norbertines, had a hard time during the religious wars and the French occupation. In the end they fled to Patershol in Ghent, which may account for the name of one street there, Drongenhof.

The neo-baroque church of St Gerolfus is also worth a visit. Although the church is 19th century, it has a number of old works of art that are so precious that thieves are always waiting to pounce. Art theft has increased so much in recent years that various parishioners have set up a church watch and take it in turns to guard the church buildings against possible thieves themselves.

✉ It is easy to reach Drongen by car via the Drongensesteenweg. The slow train to Bruges also stops there and buses leave for Drongen regularly from St Pietersstation

✉ Hundelgemsesteenweg,
Merelbeke

🚌 Bus 16, 17, 18, 19

Merelbeke

If you like beautiful scenery you do not have far to go. The country village of Merelbeke on the banks of the Scheldt is only ten minutes from Ghent at the most. Listed buildings in the vicinity include 15 castles, the Schelderode mill and the churchyard with a Calvary and a burial chapel. This rural community has a large number of nature reserves and recreation areas within its boundaries and only the main ones are mentioned below.

The mill near Merelbeke

To begin with there is the Gentbos, an area of natural woodland crossed by many footpaths.

Then there are the Makkegemse Bossen, woods which cover hundreds of hectares. These woods are an official nature reserve and public access is limited to a small area.

The Vurtzak is a wetland area with footpaths through it. You need to take care after heavy rain and it is advisable to wear strong footwear if walking here.

The Liedermeerspark has a hospital for sick birds that is open to the public and there are also a number of hides. You can visit with or without a guide but after high winds you are likely to find your way blocked by fallen trees across the paths.

Finally, in the near by village of Munte you can visit the woodland Heilig Geestgoed. However, in the shooting season, when the hunters could mistake you for game, visits are forbidden.

The Castle of Ooidonk

Do visit the village of Bachte-Maria-Leerne. It is situated beside the River Leie and because it has been blessed with a particular quality of light it became the base for many Impressionist artists, including Emile Claus. The castle of Ooidonk is undoubtedly the biggest attraction in this village.

⊠ Ooidonkdreef, Bachte-Maria-Leerne
☎ 09–2826123
🕐 Easter–15 Sep: Sun; Jul–Aug: Sat–Sun

The owner of this beautiful moated castle is Count Juan 't Kint deRoodebeke. He will be happy to welcome you there in person. The reasons for this need explanation: it is nowadays actually no joke being a count and the owner of a huge 400-year-old castle built in the Spanish Renaissance style. The building, together with a lake and 300ha of parkland, has to be maintained. Restoration is an ongoing task and the Belgian federal government is anything but generous when it comes to grants for art and listed buildings. So the count has turned his coach-house into a restaurant and bar, his castle is hired out for seminars and conferences and every year he takes about 25,000 visitors round his estate in order to keep his head above water. Heating alone costs half a million Belgian francs.

In the mainly 19th-century interior, you will enjoy seeing the unique collection of paintings, tapestries, porcelain and silver in the salons. Outside is a walled 18th-century garden, a distillery, gardens in the English style and a huge pair of wrought-iron entrance gates. Children will love to go for a drive in a carriage (Sundays only).

The castle of Ooidonk

✉ Mooring on the corner of
Coupure and Lindelei
☎ 09–2337917
⏰ Apr–Oct 10–6
🚢 Rederij Minerva

Along the Leie near St Martens-Latem and Afsnee

You must leave the car behind, forget about train or bus and get behind the wheel of a boat to travel peacefully upstream on the Leie near St Martens-Latem.

St Martens-Latem is a big name in the art world. It was the home of the Latem School of painting, and the Expressionists such as Permeke and van de Woestijne, who were world famous and whose canvases command high prices at art auctions nowadays. This little village, today the home of professors, politicians and artists, continues to present itself as an artists' village and boasts various galleries.

Leave from Coupure in the centre of Ghent. You must go slowly in order to avoid causing a wash which can cause the eggs in the ducks' nests to break against the bank. In addition you will have more time to enjoy your surroundings and save yourself a hefty fine.

The first half hour takes you past the Citadelpark (▶ 37) and the Blaarmeersen. This will give you time to get used to the handling of the boat and this form of transport. It will also take half an hour because you have to go through a narrow lock and also cross the Ringvaart, which is used by large vessels. This canal was dug to make it easier for traffic on the inland waters to reach the port of Ghent, because the low bridges in the centre of the city make that impossible. When you have survived this experience you enter another world altogether. Suddenly you are sailing among fields, past cows and weeping willows, big lime trees and quacking ducks.

There are wonderful views to be had on the meandering Leie

You very rarely meet anyone else. If you do see anyone it is most likely to be a resident of one of the Leie villages who travels by boat. There is one bend after another and from time to time you will even be held up by a small ferry that is still worked by hand.

You will not see Drongen because you turn left before you reach it. On your left you will see the beautiful 13th-century church of St Jan de Doper in Afsnee. The churchyard surrounding the church extends right up to the water's edge. This is one of the few early Gothic churches still standing. Immediately behind it is the summer residence of the writer Cyriel Buysse who died there.

Finally you come to St Martens-Latem, village of artists and millionaires. Constant Permeke, Valerius de Saedeleer, Albert Servaes, Leon de Smet and many, many others mean that this village is indissolubly linked with art and the views you see have been put on canvas innumerable times. The Leie was for the Latem School what the Seine was for the French Impressionists. It was a constant source of inspiration and you must have seen the setting to understand why.

Any adult can drive one of these motorboats without a navigation permit, provided he or she observes the speed limits and other conditions. You must always give way to commercial vessels and, as on Belgian roads, keep to the right. Boats are hired by the hour so remember you have to get back within an agreed time. You need to allow a good four hours to make the most of a trip to St Martens-Latem (or even further) keeping to the speed limits. As soon as leaves start to fall off the trees you also need to be prepared to remove branches from the propeller. But that is not difficult in practice and you don't need to worry about losing your fingers.

 St Pietersstation
Trains run to Ostend
every hour

Ostend

The Belgian coast is a good half hour from Ghent by train. The nearest seaside resort is Ostend, known as the Queen of Seaside Resorts, thanks to King Leopold II who stayed here regularly and invested a lot of money in the resort and in his country seats in the area.

In 1722 the city received a patent from Charles VI that gave it a 30-year monopoly of trade with Africa and India. This gave the place time to become wealthy and very smart. During the *fin de siècle* it was a fashionable seaside resort and the high aristocracy came here to parade along the seafront promenades. The city flourished and elegant buildings were erected. You can still see many of the gentlemens residences from this period, although sometimes they are dwarfed by the modern and rather bleak apartment blocks.

Ostend is worth a visit for the Provinviaal Museum voor Moderne Kunst (Provincial Museum of Modern Art) alone. In addition, Ostend is the city where the Anglo-Belgian artist James Ensor was born, lived and worked. If you have seen his etchings in the Ghent Museum of Fine Art you will enjoy visiting the house where his work was created. Ensor had a keen interest in the macabre, especially masks and skeletons,something you sense very strongly in the James Ensorhuis in Vlaanderenstraat.

With the second most important airport in Belgium, the ferry route to England and a large fishing port Ostend is more than simply a tourist seaside resort. You can go to the races at the elegant Wellington Racecourse, relax in the alkaline waters of the Thermal Institute, quadruple your wealth or become bankrupt in the Casino Kuursaal, eat fresh sea slugs, or stroll along the 6km of promenades and enjoy the North Sea, perhaps not so blue, but nevertheless full of character.

Where To...

Above: *law-abiding lads add their
tags to the only legal graffiti street*

Ghent

Prices

Eating in Ghent is not cheap but the prices are justified in that you are eating food that is guaranteed freshly cooked and everything is prepared to a high standard.

£ = less than BF600
££ = between BF600 and BF1,200
£££ = more than BF1,200

Restaurants & Cafés

De Acht Zaligheden (££)

Tasty and unpretentious food. The restaurant is on the bank of the River Leie.
⊠ **Oudburg 41** ☎ **09–2243197**
⏰ **Lunch and dinner. Closed Mon and Sat midday onwards**
🚊 **Krommewal**

Agora (£££)

You sit in a comfortable Lloyd-Loom chair and can enjoy all the delicacies served at a beautifully decorated table by friendly staff
⊠ **Klein Turkije 14**
☎ **09–2252558**
⏰ **Tue–Sat lunch and dinner**
🚊 **Korenmarkt**

Alexander De Grote (£)

Greek grills and typical baked dishes in a warm, cosy atmosphere. There is also a takeaway service.
⊠ **Oude Houtlei 154**
☎ **09–2335869**
⏰ **Lunch and dinner**
🚊 **Hoogstraat**

Allegro Moderato (£££)

First-rate restaurant that conjures symphonies on your plate. A splendid wine list and interior – altogether a culinary treat.
⊠ **Korenlei 7**
☎ **09–2332332** ⏰ **Tue–Sun lunch and dinner**
🚊 **Korenmarkt**

Amandeus (££)

Popular place for spare ribs, where you can eat as much as you like for a fixed price. Sometimes you need to book.
⊠ **Plotersgracht 8**
☎ **09–2251385**
⏰ **Daily dinner**
🚊 **St Veerleplein**

De Appelier (£)

One of the few vegetarian restaurants in this city. Well presented and tasty dishes at student-friendly, affordable prices.
⊠ **Citadellaan 47**
☎ **09–2216733**
⏰ **Mon–Thu, Sat lunch and dinner**
🚊 **Overpoortstraat**

Ata (£)

Eating house in Turkishtown. Particularly good selection of pizzas and lamb.
⊠ **Sleepstraat 110/A**
☎ **09–2237083**
⏰ **Daily dinner**
🚊 **Sleepstraat**

Baan Thai (££)

Belongs to one of the most notable eastern restaurants in the Low Countries. Very hot dishes are marked with a symbol on the extensive menu.
⊠ **Corduwanierstraat 57**
☎ **09–2332141**
⏰ **Daily dinner**
🚊 **St Veerleplein**

Basile (££)

Brightly decorated restaurant in the former neighbourhood of the industrial bourgeoisie. Offers quality classic and local dishes.
⊠ **Coupure Right 70**
☎ **09–2332612**
⏰ **Tue–Fri lunch and dinner**
🚊 **Annonciadestraat**

Bij den Wijzen en den Zot (£££)

Culinary *tours de force* served in this restaurant in the heart of the Patershol. For gourmets only.
⊠ **Hertogstraat 42**
☎ **09–2234230** ⏰ **Sun, Tue–Fri lunch and dinner**
🚊 **St Veerleplein**

Het Blauwe Huis (££)

Trendy eating place in a smartly decorated (blue) house. Steers a course between fast food and refinement, known nowadays as fusion cooking.

⊠ Drabstraat 17
☎ 09–2331005
🕐 Lunch and dinner. Closed Fri and Sat early afternoon
🚊 Hoogstraat

De Blauwe Kiosk (£)

The best the sea has to offer, in your hand from a stall, surrounded by the flower market. Oysters and scampi.

⊠ Kouter 🕐 Sat–Sun lunch
🚊 Kouter

De Blauwe Zalm (£££)

Although a blue salmon doesn't immediately sound appetising, this is a more than excellent restaurant in the pure Patershol tradition. The kitchen is visible from the street.

⊠ Vrouwebroersstraat 2
☎ 09–2240852
🕐 Lunch and dinner. Closed Mon and Sat early afternoon
🚊 St Veerleplein

Het Bonte Koe (£)

A good place to breakfast with the newspaper or a magazine. The interior betrays a fascination with everything to do with cows.

⊠ Keizer Karelstraat 8
☎ 09–2690620
🕐 Mon–Sat breakfast and lunch
🚊 Oude Beestenmarkt

Brasil (££)

Brazilian cuisine that is often described in the trade press as cuisine with the style of Ronaldo and the elegance of the Carnival. The staff look good too and they dance a samba at your table.

⊠ Emile Braunplein 15
☎ 09–2257597
🕐 Lunch and dinner. Closed Fri and Sat afternoon
🚊 Korenmarkt

Brasserie P. (£)

Trendy European snack bar in Turkishtown. Cosy and elegant but expensive for what you get on your plate.

⊠ Sleepstraat 65
☎ 09–2238158
🕐 Daily lunch and dinner
🚊 Sleepstraat

Brooderie (£)

Sandwich bar where smokers are not welcome. A place for the health conscious.

⊠ Jan Breydelstraat 8
☎ 09–2250623 🕐 Mon–Sat lunch 🚊 St Veerleplein

Het Buikske Vol (££)

Fashionable cuisine of course, with a view of the Leie and the Mannekin Pis, symbol of the Burgundian zest for life.

⊠ Kraanlei 17 ☎ 09–2251880
🕐 Mon–Tue, Thu–Sat lunch and dinner 🚊 St Veerleplein

Cantina Mexicana (££)

Refined and typical Mexican dishes in a warm, friendly room. A must for lovers of spicy food.

⊠ Lammerstraat 33
☎ 09–2255864 🕐 Daily dinner
🚊 Zuid

Downstairs (£)

Cheap cellar restaurant where eel, one of the Flemish dishes, has been made a speciality.

⊠ Korenmarkt 6
☎ 09–2254891
🕐 Tue–Fri, Sun lunch and dinner 🚊 Korenmarkt

Vegetarian Food

A local will usually think that as a vegetarian you are denying yourself great pleasure. Nevertheless, most restaurants will have a vegetarian dish (even if not on the menu) and will respect your eating habits. You just have to ask.

Student Restaurant
Young people with a student card can eat cheaply and well during the academic year (Oct–Jun) in the student restaurant at the university.
✉ Overpoort
🚋 Overpoort

Casa de las Tapas (££)
Spanish nibbles, but so many that they make a complete and tasty meal.
✉ Corduwanierstraat 14
☎ 09–2251889
🕓 Wed–Mon lunch and dinner
🚋 St Veerleplein

Casa España (£)
Offers typical Spanish dishes, especially paella. You can sit outside in good weather and you have a lovely view of the Gravensteen.
✉ St Veerleplein 3
☎ 09–2251889 🕓 Daily lunch and dinner 🚋 St Veerleplein

Colmar (££)
Well-known chain where you pay a certain sum at the entrance and then can eat as much as you like, from starters to sweets. This arrangement is only really interesting if you have a large appetite.
✉ Antwerpsesteenweg 1104
☎ 09–3559355
🕓 Daily lunch and dinner
🚋 Antwerpsesteenweg

Cour St Georges (Het St Jorishof) (££) (► 61)
The meals here lack a certain refinement but the name Cour St Georges has a great reputation, probably because it is the oldest hotel in Europe.
✉ Botermarkt 2 ☎ 09–2242424
🕓 Sun–Fri dinner
🚋 E. Braunplein

De Drie Biggetjes (££)
An absolutely classic restaurant managed by one of the best chefs in Flanders with years of experience in various top kitchens.
✉ Zeugsteeg 7 ☎ 09–2244648
🕓 Daily lunch and dinner
🚋 St Veerleplein

Erasmus (£)
Cosy and atmospheric place to become acquainted with Flemish cuisine; *waterzooi*, eel, casseroles and many local beers.
✉ Mageleinstraat 4
☎ 09–2251904 🕓 Sun–Fri lunch and dinner
🚋 E. Braunplein

Excelsior (££)
Quiet cosy little restaurant with a fascination for beer and where the duck breast tastes delicious.
✉ Hoogpoort 29
☎ 09–2342402 🕓 Daily lunch and dinner 🚋 St Veerleplein

Fenikshor Taverne (££)
The landlady stands at the cooker and enjoys producing one of her specialities: crown of lamb or various eel recipes. Lots of grills.
✉ Kortrijksesteenweg 857
☎ 09–2452457 🕓 Mon–Fri lunch and dinner
🚋 Kortrijksesteenweg

Fenix (£)
Snack bar with pub where they will quickly rustle up spaghetti, lasagne or a toasted sandwich.
✉ Phoenixstraat 101
☎ 09–2276506 🕓 Daily lunch and dinner 🚋 Seghersplein

Finnigans pub (£)
Irish pub offering good traditional Irish pub grub, a hefty sandwich or hot soup.
✉ Hooiaard 8 ☎ 09–2259241
🕓 Daily lunch
🚋 Korenmarkt

Florian (£)
Those with a sweet tooth will have already found their way to this lovely gentlemens house with a contemporary interior.

✉ Volderstraat 13
☎ 09–2238343 🍴 Mon–Sat breakfast and lunch
🚊 Brabantdam

De Gekroonde Hoorden (££)
Popular spare rib restaurant by the entrance to the Prinsenhof, famous for its 16th-century facade with ornate carvings of a number of Belgian princes and emperors.
✉ Burgstraat 4 ☎ 09–2333774
🍴 Daily dinner
🚊 St Veerleplein

Het Gents Fonduehuisje (££)
Fondue symbolises a sociable way of eating which is certainly the case in this pleasant establishment.
✉ Jan Breydelstraat 30
☎ 09–2343405 🍴 Daily dinner
🚊 St Veerleplein

The Ghost (££)
Ghent *waterzooi* in the oldest crypt in Belgium, with a view of the three towers.
✉ Korenlei 24 ☎ 09–2258902
🍴 Fri–Tue lunch and dinner
🚊 Korenmarkt

Goossens (£££)
Culinary family restaurant that makes a point of being child-friendly. The menu has seven courses.
✉ Kortrijksesteenweg 198
☎ 09–2811100 🍴 Tue–Fri lunch and dinner
🚊 Kortrijksesteenweg

Graaf Van Egmond (£)
Historic building where the humanists once sought refuge and where today you can taste local specialities (especially *waterzooi*) at competitive prices.
✉ St Michielsplein 21
☎ 09–2250727 🍴 Daily lunch and dinner 🚊 Korenmarkt

Le Grand Bleu (£)
You can guess from the name – this is the place for lobster and fish dishes. Considering the prices lunch especially is well worthwhile.
✉ Snepkaai 15 ☎ 09–2205025
🍴 Sun–Fri lunch and dinner
🚊 St Denijslaan

De Gustibus (££)
Plain decor where you will find an elegant meal well prepared at a reasonable price. The calves' sweetbreads are highly recommended.
✉ Bennesteeg 8
☎ 09–2330298 🍴 Daily lunch and dinner 🚊 E. Braunplein

Le Hommard Rouge (£££)
A well-hidden restaurant where the food and eating are taken seriously.
✉ Ketelvest 9 ☎ 09–2338703
🍴 Daily lunch and dinner
🚊 Nederkouter

Jan Van Den Bon (£££)
However good the restaurants of Ghent this is the only one that earned a star in the prestigious *Michelin Guide*. Rightly, in fact. You can eat less well for more money in many places.
✉ Koning Leopold II–laan 43
☎ 09–2219085 🍴 Tue–Fri dinner 🚊 Citadelpark

Chez Jean (££)
Delicious food at the foot of the St Niklaaskerk. Walls are lined with wines that will make your mouth water. At midday businessmen with briefcases and mobile phones sit here having lunch.
✉ Cataloniëstraat 3
☎ 09–2233040 🍴 Lunch and dinner. Closed Mon afternoon and Sat 🚊 Korenmarkt

Chip Stalls
Chips: world famous and often the subject of Belgian jokes. You really cannot leave Belgium without visiting a chip stall at least once. Alas, competition with American-style fast food restaurants is very keen and frozen chips are gaining ground. The sad custom of serving chips with everything applies to restaurants and gives the visitor the impression that in the Belgian home nothing else is cooked but chips. Belgians themselves prefer to eat their chips at a chip stall, often to provide 'blotting paper' before getting down to some serious beer drinking. Everyone swears by their own favourite chip stall but **Mia De Jaegers** on the **Vrijdagmarkt** seems to be the choice of most local people. Ghent is also the place where people were crazy enough to run a lorry on cooking oil and, yes, it worked.

Patershol
If you want to dine out in one of the many restaurants in the Patershol you will need to book a table in advance.

Karel De Stoute (££)
In the summer you feast in the courtyard garden and in the winter you eat by the open fire in this 17th-century aristocrats house.
✉ Vrouwebroersstraat 5
☎ 09–2241735
🕐 Lunch and dinner; closed Wed and Sat afternoon
🚊 St Veerleplein

Keizershor (£)
Eccentric, contemporary brasserie. Very tasty food but can sometimes be pretty busy.
✉ Vrijdagmarkt 47
☎ 09–2234446 🕐 Mon–Fri dinner 🚊 Bij St Jacobs

't Keteltje (£)
Salad bar, rolls, and various snacks on the bridge over the Ketelvest. From the terrace you can watch drivers becoming agitated on their way to the city centre.
✉ Nederkouter 1
☎ 09–2332255 🕐 Daily lunch
🚊 Nederkouter

't Klockhuys (££)
The interior is full of clocks that tell the wrong time. The kitchen is the same as that of Het Buikske Vol and is run by the same people.
✉ Corduwanierstraat 65
☎ 09–2234241
🕐 Tue–Sun lunch and dinner
🚊 St Veerleplein

K-Roes-L (£)
Snack bar serving hefty buckwheat pancakes; they are filled with fresh, nutritious Belgian vegetables and other fillings to the customer's choice.
✉ Oudburg 37
☎ 09–2240233
🕐 Daily lunch and dinner
🚊 Krommewal

De Kruik (£££)
This is a 13th-century wine cellar that nowadays is the fish restaurant of choice for people from Ghent and the surrounding area.
✉ Donkersteeg 5
☎ 09–2257101
🕐 Mon–Wed, Fri–Sat lunch and dinner
🚊 Korenmarkt

Lucifer (££)
In this DIY restaurant you have to cook your own food on the lava grill; fun to do with the children or on an evening out with friends.
✉ Belfortstraat 31
☎ 09–2339197
🕐 Daily lunch and dinner
🚊 Bij St Jacobs

Lunch Garden (£)
The restaurant of a department store chain, designed for people who want to shop for a long time and fancy something more than a snack in between.
✉ Korenmarkt 3
☎ 09–2256080
🕐 Mon–Sat lunch
🚊 Korenmarkt

Mercatro Café-Restaurant (£)
You can enjoy anything from a little snack to the menu of the month. All this in pleasant surroundings at a reasonable price.
✉ Kliniekstraat 68, Gentbrugge
☎ 09–2308911
🕐 All days of the week

The Moka (£)
Restaurant with friendly service and delicious salmon dishes. Pub-like interior.
✉ Koestraat 46
☎ 09–2250054
🕐 Mon–Fri dinner
🚊 Kouter

Mosquito Coast (££)
Café-cum-eatery for world travellers. International drinks and snacks. The attic houses a small dining area with a sultry Asian atmosphere.
- ✉ Serpentstraat 5
- ☎ 09–2243720
- 🕐 Daily lunch and dinner
- 🚌 Bij St Jacobs

Myconos (£)
Greek restaurant where you don't need to dance the Zorba between the main course and the sweet.
- ✉ Vlaanderenstraat 13
- ☎ 09–2243036 🕐 Daily dinner
- 🚌 Vlaanderenstraat

Het Oeverloze Eiland (£)
Friendly service and unique decor in which to enjoy an aperitif with a snack or a sensually stimulating desert.
- ✉ Oudburg 39 ☎ 09–2343200
- 🕐 Daily 🚌 Krommewal

Oranjerie (££)
Creative dishes in pleasant surroundings. The menu is changed completely every month of the year.
- ✉ Corduwanierstraat 6
- ☎ 09–2241008 🕐 Thu–Mon dinner 🚌 St Veerleplein

Othello (£££)
Delicatessen and restaurant where everything involves wine. There is an impressive vinothèque.
- ✉ Ketelvest 8 ☎ 09–2330009
- 🕐 Tue–Wed, Sat–Sun lunch and dinner 🚌 Nederkouter

Pablo's Gent nv (£) (► 39)
Part of an international chain offering Mexican food and drink only.
- ✉ Kleine Vismarkt 2
- ☎ 09–2337151 🕐 Tue–Sun lunch and dinner
- 🚌 St Veerleplein

Pakhuis (££)
This fantastic location is a huge loft, contained in a former warehouse of the old port of Ghent. You can just have something to eat or drink at the bar.
- ✉ Schuurkenstraat 4
- ☎ 09–2235555 🕐 Sun–Thu lunch and dinner
- 🚌 Korenmarkt

't Palinghuisje (££)
A huge buffet of eel dishes for those who can never have enough of this wonderful Flemish speciality.
- ✉ Plotersgracht 2
- ☎ 09–2250814 🕐 Wed–Mon dinner 🚌 St Veerleplein

Sparerib Caffee (££)
Yet another place specialising in spare ribs although this breaks with the tradition of a fixed price for as much as you can eat.
- ✉ Kraanlei 19 ☎ 09–2333001
- 🕐 Tue–Sun dinner
- 🚌 St Veerleplein

Sobrie (£)
You can immerse yourself in more than 40 years of skill in the world of Ghent pastry cooks. Try the applejack, the *gentenaar* or a *stropke*.
- ✉ Mageleinstraat 46
- ☎ 09–2251019 🕐 Wed–Mon lunch 🚌 E. Braunplein

St Pietersstation (££)
If you get hungry while waiting for a train you can go to the station buffet with its grand café atmosphere. Also does breakfast.
- ✉ Koningin Maria Hendrikaplein ☎ 09–2200864
- 🕐 Daily lunch and dinner
- 🚌 St Pietersstation

The Solitary Eater
The solitary eater is one of the poetic icons of the city. He or she has breakfast or lunch in the pub behind the newspaper or the magazine that most eating places offer, and in the evening is used to going to a restaurant and having a chat with the man or women behind another newspaper. Breakfast in a pub is a good way to make informal contacts.

Credit Cards
Credit cards are accepted in most restaurants including: American Express, Diners Club, Visa and Eurocard.

Tête-à-tête (£)
Extremely reliable French cuisine with a pleasant terrace by the River Leie and a view of the Onthoofdingsbrug.
📧 Jan Breydelstraat 32
🕾 09–2339500 🔘 Wed–Sun lunch and dinner
🚌 St Veerleplein

Tokyo (££)
The only restaurant in East Flanders where traditional Japanese dishes are served.
📧 Zwijnaardsesteenweg 130
🕾 09–2211370 🔘 Daily dinner
🚌 Zwijnaardsesteenweg

Trio's (££)
Local Ghent specialities. Family recipes handed down through the generations.
📧 Donkersteeg 26
🕾 09–2251590 🔘 Thu–Tue lunch and dinner
🚌 E. Braunplein

Urga (£)
As well as a Russian music venue this new trendy restaurant is also known as a vodka temple and a jolly place where you can get your teeth into a Russian dish.
📧 Kartuizerlaan 105
🕾 09–2252945 🔘 Thu–Tue dinner 🚌 Tolhuislaan

De Vier Tafels (££)
Splendid and much cherished restaurant. There are more than four tables and the dishes and the drinks come from all corners of the globe.
📧 Plotersgracht 6
🕾 09–2250525
🔘 Daily lunch and dinner
🚌 St Veerleplein

Virus (££)
Forms part of De Vier Tafels and specialises in ostrich,

crocodile and muskrat.
📧 Corduwaniersstraat 9
🕾 09–2250525 🔘 Daily lunch and dinner 🚌 St Veerleplein

Walry's (£)
This is a literary café but between the bookshelves you can have the best pancakes in Ghent or a nutritious snack.
📧 Zwijnaardsesteenweg 6
🕾 09–2200018 🔘 Mon–Sat lunch 🚌 Zwijnaardsesteenweg

Pubs

Bal Infernal
Nicely set up pub that attracts twenty-somethings.
📧 Kammerstraat 6 🕾 09–2331403 🚌 Bij St Jacobs

Bar-Bier
This barber has found the ideal combination; he cuts your hair while you have a peaceful beer in the pub.
📧 St Margrietstraat 18 🕾 09–2234593 🚌 Ziekenhuizen

Bellemanpub
The bellman is the town-crier of Ghent. He brings people up to date with events in the city with his loud voice and a bell. This is his base.
📧 Botermarkt 8 🕾 09–2240152
🚌 E. Braunplein

't Dreupelkot
Tiny pub that can generate a lot of music when the guests have drunk enough gin.
📧 Groentenmarkt 9
🕾 09–2242120 🚌 St Veerleplein

De Dulle Griet (► 55)
Bar aimed particularly at tourists, ideal place for getting to know the huge range of Belgian beers on offer.

✉ **Vrijdagmarkt 50**
☎ 09–2242455
🚋 Bij St Jacobs

De Grote Avond
A pub-cum-café in which to chat, stuffed full of old ad posters and other kitsch.
✉ **Huidevetterskaai 40**
☎ 09–2243121
🚋 Sleepstraat

Den Hemel
Folk pub serving Irish and Belgian beers. Now and then there are live performances in the small space.
✉ **Muinkkaai 120**
☎ 09–2336690
🚋 St Pietersplein

l'Heure Bleue
Hearty night owls often make this trendy bar their last port of call just before the last chairs are put up on the tables.
✉ **Bij St Jacobs 11**
☎ 09–2242020
🚋 Bij St Jacobs

Hotsy Totsy
Literary café run by relatives of Hugo Claus, all in the style of the 1950s. Very rarely a membership card is issued.
✉ **Hoogstraat 1** ☎ 09–2242012
🚋 Hoogstraat

Hungaria
Hungarian pub-cum-restaurant, for a drink with fiddle music, or a hefty plate of goulash.
✉ **Hoogpoort 41**
☎ 09–2232064
🚋 E. Braunplein

Manteca Jazzcafé
Pub with modern decor and the accent on Latin-American jazz. The Salsa is danced regularly, come and watch the fast-moving feet.

✉ **Catal.oniëstraat 2**
☎ 09–2341263
🚋 Korenmarkt

De Muze
A café with art gallery in which to chat. Meeting place for many Sunday painters and others from Ghent.
✉ **Rekelingestraat 3**
☎ 09–2307404
🚋 St Veerleplein

Paradox
Trendy club for gays and lesbians with a fragrant and pleasant bar where they serve a wonderful cup of coffee.
✉ **Vlaanderenstraat 22**
☎ 09–2337040
🚋 Vlaanderenstraat

Pink Flamingo's
Kitsch pub stuffed full of images of the Virgin Mary, beer mats, prayer cards and everything that other people keep on the mantelpiece or in the attic. Busy but very pleasant.
✉ **Onderstraat 55**
☎ 09–2334718
🚋 Bij St Jacobs

Platte Beurs
Lively pub that attracts a very young clientele to an often hearty atmosphere.
✉ **Klein Turkije 20**
☎ 09–2250831
🚋 Korenmarkt

Pole–Pole
In Afrikaans the name means 'at ease'. Luxurious cocktail bar visited by fanatical Africa travellers. Also has its own festival and travel club.
✉ **Lammerstraat 8**
☎ 09–3553400
🚋 Zuid

Breastfeeding
Pubs and restaurants that have a room set apart where mothers can breastfeed in peace display a blue sticker at the entrance with a nursing mother on it.

De Roode Piano
Roguish pub where, given the amount drunk, people dance on the piano more than they play it.
- ✉ Belfortstraat 26
- ☎ 09–2250360
- 🚊 Bij St Jacobs

Sioux
Dark and kitsch pub with a small dance floor between the prison bars. The venue is often hired for all kinds of parties.
- ✉ Platteberg 8
- ☎ 09–2337183
- 🚊 Zuid

Skoop
Sister cinema of a Scandinavian film house with an extremely friendly pub full of, naturally, old film posters and photos of the stars of the silver screen over the years.
- ✉ St Annaplein 63
- ☎ 09–2333258
- 🚊 Zuid

Sphinx Café
Cinema café-cum-pub with film music playing in the background. Anyone can go there but it is mainly the haunt of cinema-goers from the Sphinx Cinema who want to chat over a drink afterwards.
- ✉ St Michielshelling 4
- ☎ 09–2256086
- 🚊 Korenmarkt

De Tempelier
Calls to mind the atmosphere of medieval chivalry but more suitable as a place to dive into the list of beers.
- ✉ Meerseniersstraat 9
- ☎ 09–2251740
- 🚊 Bij St Jacobs

Tolhuisje (► 67)
This place certainly qualifies for the title of the smallest café in Ghent. In the summer the terrace is packed with visitors from the famous Graslei and people who want to enjoy the sun.
- ✉ Graslei 11 ☎ 09–2243090
- 🚊 Korenmarkt

't Trollekelderke
Pleasant dark place in the land of the trolls. Perfect for someone who wants to have a peaceful night out.
- ✉ Bij St Jacobs 17
- ☎ 09–2237696
- 🚊 Bij St Jacobs

Twieoo
This place has something of the air of a parish hall in a village, the glitter ball above the dance floor is almost a valuable antique, but anyone who dances here with his eyes shut won't be bothered by it.
- ✉ Overpoortstraat 9 ☎ 09–2212221 🚊 St Pietersplein

't Velootje
A monkish type receives his guest by the open fire and only serves you if he feels like it. It is more a stable than a pub and is full of cycles and statues of saints. Tourists love it.
- ✉ Kalversteeg 2 ☎ 09–2232834 🚊 Krommewal

Het Waterhuis aan de Bierkant
One of the Ghent pubs with the express ambition of having the biggest collection of Belgian beers on the menu.
- ✉ Groentenmarkt 9
- ☎ 09–2250680
- 🚊 St Veerleplein

Restaurants Outside Ghent

Bruges

Het Dagelijks Brood (£)
Het Dagelijks Brood not only sells fresh bread and cakes but you can eat them at a long wooden table. The menu includes salads, sandwiches and extensive Tuscan lunches.
✉ Philipstockstraat 21
☎ 050–336050 ⊙ Closed Tue

La Dentellière (££)
This restaurant near the Minnewater is well known for its local dishes and good steaks.
✉ Wijngaardstraat 33
☎ 050–331898 ⊙ Closed Tue

Toermalijn (££)
Flemish cuisine is not designed with vegetarians in mind. It is only in the large cities that you will find vegetarian restaurants. Tourmalijn in the Alfa-Dante is one of them. Lunch and dinner are served.
✉ Coupure 29A
☎ 050–340194

Ostend

Den Artiest (£)
Traditional pub with live music, dark woodwork and art gallery. Nice surroundings for an evening chat.
✉ Kapucijnenstraat 13
☎ 059–808889

Antwerp

Allegria (££)
Artistic restaurant, menu is printed on a music score, and young musicians provide the atmosphere. You can admire or buy the paintings on the walls. Also has outstanding vegetarian cuisine.
✉ Nassaustraat 15
☎ 03–2313158
⊙ Dinner
🚋 4, 7

Fairfood (££)
A green restaurant with a strongly vegetarian menu. There is lamb and chicken for meat eaters.
✉ Graaf Van Egmontstraat 60
☎ 03–2389296 ⊙ Wed–Mon lunch and dinner 🚋 4, 8

Hoffy's Take Away (££)
A Jewish restaurant where they are happy to initiate tourists into the kosher traditions of Eastern European, Sephardic, Ashenazic and Israeli dishes. Also takeaway.
✉ Lange Kievitstraat 52
☎ 03–2343535
⊙ Sun–Thu lunch and dinner, Fri lunch 🚋 2, 15

Noord (££)
Café-brasserie in an authentic Gothic building with a huge terrace. Large portions of Flemish dishes.
✉ Grote Markt 24
☎ 03–2322816 ⊙ Daily lunch and dinner 🚋 2, 11, 15

Pelgrom (£)
Pub-restaurant in medieval style in interconnecting 15th-century cellars. Waiters are dressed in the style of Brueghel. Dishes are prepared strictly according to medieval recipes. Very popular with tourists.
✉ Pelgrimstraat 15
☎ 03–2340809 ⊙ Daily lunch and dinner 🚋 2, 11, 15

Sushi Factory (£)
Super-clean minimalist restaurant with takeaway. Specialities to taste from BF45 a piece and huge menus of ready-made sushi with a glass of Japanese beer.
✉ Nationalestraat 54
☎ 03–2130300 ⊙ Daily lunch and dinner 🚋 2, 15

Price Reductions
At the tourist information office (Belfort) you can obtain a list of shops, hotels and restaurants. If you make an arrangement via any of the hotels on the list you can claim a number of vouchers for price reductions at shops and museums.

Pub Crawls
Pub crawls are organised regularly. During Whit weekend there is a big jazz pub crawl. The names of pubs taking part are shown on posters in the city.

Where to Stay

Prices

Ghent is known as one of the most expensive places to stay in Europe. The guide prices in this book refer to a double room for one night, including breakfast, during the holiday season.

£ = less than BF3,000
££ = between BF3,000 and BF6,000
£££ = more than BF6,000

Adoma (£)

The cheapest 3-star hotel in the city, near the station and ideal for visitors to exhibitions.

✉ **St Denijslaan 19**
☎ **09–2226550**
🚇 **St Denijslaan**

Alfa Flanders (£££)

This lovely 4-star hotel is between St Pietersstation and the centre. Offers clients a card for public transport or a bicycle.

✉ **Koning-Albertlaan 121**
☎ **09–2226065**
🚇 **St Pietersstation**

Ascona (£)

Very friendly family establishment between the station and the junction of the E17 and E40. There are attractive weekend reductions, certainly for single rooms.

✉ **Voskenslaan 105**
☎ **09–2212756**
🚇 **St Pietersstation**

Astoria (££)

Offers a pleasant stay in comfortable rooms. In the morning a fresh breakfast buffet awaits you in the light and rustic eating area.

✉ **Achilles Musschestraat 39**
☎ **09–2228413**
🚇 **St Pietersstation**

Boatel (££)

Five lovely standard rooms and two luxury rooms on a boat. A unique hotel experience on the last straight section of the River Leie.

✉ **Voorhoutkaai 29A**
☎ **09–2671030** 🚇 **Dampoort**

Campanile Gent (£)

Guests are given passes for the most important museums and exhibitions (in low season) and the third night is free.

✉ **Akkerhage 1**
☎ **09–2200222**
🚇 **De Sterre**

Camping 'Blaarmeersen' (£)

Campsite 5km from the city for tent, caravan or camper van. There is a shop, restaurant, swimming pool, squash and tennis courts and public transport to and from the city.

✉ **Zuiderlaan 12**
☎ **09–2215399**
🚇 **Watersportbaan**

Castelnou (££)

In this hotel you stay in an apartment with sitting room, kitchenette, bedroom and bathroom and yet you can enjoy full hotel service. The longer you stay the cheaper it becomes.

✉ **Kasteellaan 51**
☎ **09–2350411**
🚇 **Dampoort**

Chamade (££)

Medium-sized hotel near the St Pietersstation, most suitable for people who are using Ghent as a stopover and want to get away early in the morning.

✉ **Blankenbergestraat 2**
☎ **09–2201515** ⏰ **Daily.**
Closed 24 Dec and 1 Jan
🚇 **St Pietersstation**

De Draecke (£)

Budget-friendly youth hostel in a quiet and picturesque part of the city. The 27 rooms have en suite facilities. Large and the best alternative for back-packers.

✉ **St Widostraat 11**
☎ **09–2337050**
🚇 **St Veerleplein**

Eden (££)
Three-star hotel on the edge of the (safe) red light district of Ghent. Ideal for anyone who often has to travel by tram or bus.
- ✉ Zuidstationstraat 24
- ☎ 09–2235151 🚋 Zuid

Europahotel (££)
Considering its 3 stars this is a very reasonably priced hotel with some good facilities, recommended for anyone wanting half board.
- ✉ Gordunakaai 59
- ☎ 09–2226071
- 🚋 Koning-Albertlaan

Flandria Centrum (£)
Cheap, friendly and very charming small family hotel in the narrow streets in the shadow of the cathedral.
- ✉ Barrestraat 3
- ☎ 09–2230626
- 🚋 Oude Beestenmarkt

Formule 1 (£)
Without a doubt the cheapest hotel in Ghent, and also the only hotel where there is no difference in price between high and low season and where a third bed is free.
- ✉ Vliegtuiglaan 21
- ☎ 09–2516310
- 🚋 Haven-Grootdok

Holiday Inn Gent UZ (£££)
A top class hotel a long way from the centre discovered a while ago by the business and artistic world. It is well placed near the most important road junctions.
- ✉ Akkerhage 2 ☎ 09–2225885
- 🚋 Universitair Ziekenhuis

Ibis Gent Centrum Kathedraal (££)
This is one of the best hotels in the city as regards price–quality ratio. 120 rooms 50m from *The Adoration of the Mystic Lamb* and the cathedral.
- ✉ Limburgstraat 2
- ☎ 09–2330000
- 🚋 E. Braunplein

Ibis Gent Centrum Opera (£)
This Ibis hotel has 14 rooms, but because it is ten minutes walk further away from the centre than the previous Ibis hotel it is rather cheaper.
- ✉ Nederkouter 24
- ☎ 09–2250707
- 🚋 Nederkouter

New Carlton Gent (£)
This hotel belonging to a well-known chain has just been renovated and has 21 rooms with all you would expect in a comparable hotel.
- ✉ Koningin-Astridlaan 138
- ☎ 09–2228836
- 🚋 St Pietersstation

St Jorishof (Cour St Georges) (££) (➤ 61)
In Europe's oldest hotel you enter the atmosphere of the historic heyday and the guild of the crossbow archers. Downstairs there is a large popular restaurant.
- ✉ Botermarkt 2
- ☎ 09–2242424
- 🚋 E. Braunplein

Soritel Gent Belfort (£££)
Four-star hotel in the tourist centre of the city. 127 rooms with all the works. An historic facade has been incorporated into the modern building. During the film festival in October many stars stay here.
- ✉ Hoogpoort 63
- ☎ 09–2333331
- 🚋 E. Braunplein

Reservations
Expansion of hotel accommodation in Ghent has not kept pace with the increase in visitor numbers. There is regularly a great shortage of beds in Ghent, especially before the Ghent Festival at the end of July when you should book well in advance. The hundreds of participating artists alone are looking for accommodation for the ten days.

Children and Pets
Most hotels provide a babysitting service and welcome pets. Wheelchair users will rarely find specially adapted toilets, not even if the hotel is advertised as being wheelchair friendly.

Where to Shop in Ghent

Free Shopping Bus
Because the city centre is a car-free zone and trades people suffer, a free shuttle bus for shoppers operates at the weekend during the Christmas period. This takes you in no time from parking 8 at Flanders Expo (St Denijs-Westrem) to the centre of Ghent. For information, telephone:
☎ 09-2109491.

Department Stores and Shopping Centres

Ava
Large department store with paper goods only. For decorated envelopes and just the right paper for tearful love letters, to files and business stationary.
✉ **Korte Meer 14**
☎ **09–2241378**
🕐 **Mon–Sat 10–6**
🚋 **Kouter**

Braempoort
Small covered shopping centre with a bar in the central courtyard. Very popular with senior citizens for a pancake and coffee.
✉ **Corner Vlaanderenstraat and Brabantdam**
🕐 **Mon–Sat 10–6**
🚋 **L. Bauwensplein**

Colruyt
Large general department store especially strong on food. If you can prove that you could buy the same product elsewhere for less, they alter their prices straight away.
✉ **Drongensesteenweg 197**
☎ **09–2266979**
🕐 **Mon–Sat 10–6**
🚋 **Drongensesteenweg**

Di
The department store for body care. From very cheap to luxurious perfumes, shampoos, night creams, combs and wash mitts.
✉ **Vrijdagmarkt 53**
☎ **09–2257744** 🕐 **Mon–Sat 10–6** 🚋 **Bij St Jacobs**

Fnac
Three floors of music, books, photographic material and multimedia.

✉ **Veldstraat 1** ☎ **09–2251042**
🕐 **Mon–Sat 10–6**
🚋 **Veldstraat**

Inno
Up the escalators from one theme to another: trinkets, lingerie, jewellery, childrens rooms and much more.
✉ **Veldstraat 86**
☎ **09–2255865**
🕐 **Mon–Sat 10–6**
🚋 **Veldstraat**

Katherine Bouckaert
Decorative and practical items for house furnishing, including a good collection of vases.
✉ **Walpoortstraat 26**
☎ **09–2236193** 🚋 **5, 50**

Pii–Pii
Original and rare foreign ornaments and silver jewellery.
✉ **Penshuisje 5–6, Groentenmarkt**
☎ **09–22233022**

Shopping Centre Gent Zuid
11,000sq m of covered shopping space, 36 shops, fashion shows and animation. Up to 13,000 different brand names.
✉ **W. Wilsonplein 4**
☎ **09–2341277**
🕐 **Mon–Sat 10–7** 🚋 **Zuid**

The Fallen Angel
Antique toys, old postcards and beautiful prayer cards.
✉ **Jan Breydelstraat 29**
☎ **09–2239415**
🚋 **1, 10, 11, 12, 13**

Veldstraat (▶ 69)
Survive the tram that clangs over the cobbles here and spend hours strolling from one large shop to the other.
🚋 **Veldstraat**

Art & Antiques

The Australian Shop
As well as trendy Australian raincoats and didgeridoos you can also buy pointillist aboriginal art.
- ✉ **Lammerstraat 4A**
- ☎ **09–2243093**
- ☐ **Zuid**

Bij St Jacobs
On Friday mornings there is a lot of noise and rushing about on this little square. Among all the junk there is always some valuable antique worth having.
- ✉ **Bij St Jacobs**
- ☐ **Bij St Jacobs**

Bonaffé
Women who would like to have a portrait of themselves in the nude can make an appointment with someone who has made the female form his profession.
- ✉ **Ajuinlei 12**
- ☎ **09–2341473**
- ☐ **Koophandelsplein**

De Buck S.& H.
Large colourful gallery with a lot of contemporary art, together with jewellery and silver.
- ✉ **Zuidstationstraat 25**
- ☎ **09–2251081**
- ☐ **Zuid**

Castle Antiques
A haven for lovers of English furniture, silver and decorative objects.
- ✉ **Burgstraat 129**
- ☎ **09–2237173**
- ☐ **St Veerleplein**

Copyright
This exclusive art bookshop also sells artistic knick-knacks as a sideline.
- ✉ **Jakobijnenstraat 8**
- ☎ **09–2235794**
- ☐ **Hoogstraat**

Foncke Richard
The deepest wish of young contemporary artists is to have a picture hung in this well-known gallery, where many of their predecessors were discovered.
- ✉ **St Jansvest 18**
- ☎ **09–2238128**
- ☐ **Brabantdam**

Het Gravensteen
Antique firm in the shadow of the Gravensteen, selling Flemish and French furniture, all kinds of old objets d'art and 16th-century copper ware.
- ✉ **Burgstraat 65**
- ☎ **09–2244645**
- ☐ **St Veerleplein**

Horta
This shop is intended as homage to the great architect, Victor Horta. In this design and interior decor business you can find a tasteful object and/or suitable design for your home.
- ✉ **St Annaplein 73**
- ☎ **09–2253935**
- ☐ **Zuid**

Museum voor Schone Kunsten (► 53)
You can find all kinds of artistic gadgets and books in the museum shop. Do take your wallet with you.
- ✉ **Citadelpark**
- ☎ **09–2221703**
- ☐ **Citadelpark**

Taillieu & Taillieu
A gallery in a wonderful gentlemans house that boasts the well-known film director and painter Peter Greenaway among its clients.
- ✉ **Fortlaan 17**
- ☎ **09–2220033**
- ☐ **Citadelpark**

Art in the City
Not least under the influence of the conservator Jan Hoet, Ghent has made a point of treating art as of paramount importance. Frequently at odds with convention the city offers the unpredictable in art, often in places where you would least expect it.

Clothing and Accessories

Lace

Cities with begijnhofs such as Bruges and Ghent (► 24) are the foremost places to buy lace garments. You will find luxury childrens garments made of lace in the Kuip. You could try this well-known outlet:

Kloskanthuis
- ✉ Korenlei 3
- ☎ 09–2236093
- 🚊 Korenmarkt

Baccarat

Large shop full of temptation. Lingerie, nightwear and swimwear to suit every taste: casual, sporty, sensual, trendy.
- ✉ Brabantdam 18
- ☎ 09–2234577
- 🚊 Kouter

Blue Velvet

For large and small, tall and short, from XS to XXL.
- ✉ Baudelostraat 19
- ☎ 09–2238017
- 🚊 Bij St Jacobs

Boothill

Sturdy clothing for the outlaw, mainly road gear and new wave clothing.
- ✉ KortrijkSepoortstraat 9
- ☎ 09–2334483
- 🚊 KortrijkSepoort

Cayenne

Trendy fashion accessories and clothing from the fashion houses that are patronised by the British Royal Family.
- ✉ Brabantdam 61
- ☎ 09–2690355
- 🚊 Kouter

Company Store

Sells jeans and everything to do with jeans: belts, tops, suitable shirts, all at reasonable prices.
- ✉ Cataloniëstraat 4
- ☎ 09–2253645
- 🚊 Korenmarkt

Den Tumi

Not for the narrow-minded, this shop is the place to go if you hanker after a beautiful tattoo or one of those essential piercings. You will also find jewellery here.
- ✉ Bagattenstraat 175
- ☎ 09–2337696
- 🚊 Nederkouter

Gris

Plain but fashionable and elegant ladies' wear with the emphasis on shades of grey.
- ✉ St Niklaasstraat 19
- ☎ 09–2243628
- 🚊 Korenmarkt

Ill'Mus

Small friendly shop with lovely elegant party wear. Nice but pricey.
- ✉ Jan Breydelstraat 18
- ☎ 09–2334090
- 🚊 St Veerleplein

In de 100:000 broeken

Anyone who has been searching for years for a particular pair of trousers should try this shop.
- ✉ Zwijnaardsesteenweg 147
- ☎ 09–2222438
- 🚊 Zwijnaardsesteenweg

In Wear

Luxury leisure wear and suits. There are two shops, one for ladies and one for gentlemen.
- ✉ Kouter 138
- ☎ 09–2238955
- 🚊 Kouter

Janssens

Beautiful shop with fashion fabrics and materials, a mecca for anyone who is creating their own clothes. Colourful, luxurious and a feast for the senses.
- ✉ Korenlei 5
- ☎ 09–2339445
- 🚊 Korenmarkt

Laundry Retail

Rails with exclusively black and white garments in an interior of ice-cold industrial design.
- ✉ Hoornstraat 3
- ☎ 09–2332821
- 🚊 Veldstraat

Mayfair
You can try on the very latest fashion shoes to the beat of deafening music.
- ✉ **Volderstraat 11**
- ☎ **09–2330389**
- 🚊 **Veldstraat**

McGregor
In 1921 invented the term 'original sportswear'. This menswear shop offers an exciting collection for the sporty businessman.
- ✉ **Brabantdam 12**
- ☎ **09–2336017**
- 🚊 **Kouter**

Mieke Muis
Second-hand childrens clothing, mainly good-quality and originally expensive.
- ✉ **St Pietersplein 21**
- ☎ **09–2229950**
- 🚊 **St Pietersplein**

Movies
Sport fashion. The decor is reminiscent of an American road movie. It is a shame that the staff seem to confuse 'cool' with indifference.
- ✉ **St Pietersnieuwstraat 5**
- ☎ **09–2242357**
- 🚊 **Zuid**

Parel
From the smallest fresh-water pearl to pearls from the South Seas and Tahiti, to suit every pocket, trendy or traditional. Experts find which jewellery best suits your style and clothes.
- ✉ **Graslei 2A**
- ☎ **09–2342031**
- 🚊 **Korenmarkt**

Ri–Kiki
Trendy (sports) shoes and boots with platform and boot soles for a young clientele or those who want to go on looking young.
- ✉ **St Pietersnieuwstraat 82**
- ☎ **09–2233022**
- 🚊 **5, 50**

Twice as Nice
Second-hand shop where often you can pick up very expensive labels for a song. Second hand but first class.
- ✉ **Dampoortstraat 72**
- ☎ **09–2330690**
- 🚊 **Dampoort**

Twiggy
Shop aimed at the contemporary woman. Personal fashion advice and a wide range of top labels, accessories and shoes.
- ✉ **Langemunt 36**
- ☎ **09–2239566**
- 🚊 **St Veerleplein**

De Witte Uil
Hippie clothing and ornaments, generally imported from Nepal and the surrounding area.
- ✉ **Jan van Stopenberghestraat 1**
- ☎ **09–2231638**
- 🚊 **Korenmarkt**

Yann
Jewellery described, in the words of the shop's own publicity, as 'splendid, unique, unforgettable, this is the only one that exists'.
- ✉ **F. Laurentplein 47**
- ☎ **09–2336093**
- 🚊 **Vlaanderenstraat**

Books, CDs & Records

Strip Cartoons

Belgian artists are renowned for strip cartoons, the most famous export being *Tintin*; and as far as the so-called 'ninth art' is concerned, the flag is still flying high. You can see that Belgium is the country of strip cartoons from the number of specialist bookshops.

Adhemar

This shop, named after a character in a Belgian strip carton, sells exclusively – you've guessed it – strip cartoons.

- ✉ Kammerstraat 25
- ☎ 09–2243239
- 🚇 Bij St Jacobs

Audivox

Business specialising in English literature, always has a stock of books which have recently been filmed.

- ✉ St Pietersnieuwstraat 15
- ☎ 09–2242488
- 🚇 Zuid

Bilbo

The cheapest chain for radio and chart pop music.

- ✉ Overpoortstraat 57
- ☎ 09–2226365
- 🚇 Citadelpark

Betty Boop

As well as famous and rare strip cartoons also stocks enjoyable gimmicks and other interesting games.

- ✉ Overpoortstraat 110
- ☎ 09–2220576
- 🚇 Citadelpark

Copyright

The shop only stocks art books. Includes titles from all over the world, from prehistoric to contemporary art, monographs and biographies of artists.

- ✉ Jacobijnenstraat 8
- ☎ 09–2235794
- 🚇 Hoogstraat

The Dance Solution

Small shop specialising in contemporary dance and club music. Frequented by DJs.

- ✉ Steendam 72
- ☎ 09–2251165
- 🚇 Dampoort

Fried Chicken Records

One of the rare shops where you can still find vinyl.

- ✉ Nederkouter 47
- ☎ 09–2231627
- 🚇 Nederkouter

Herkenrath

Lovely bookshop that has acquired a place in Belgian literary history. A number of years ago distinguished authors were regular visitors Mainly French literature stocked.

- ✉ Veldstraat 43
- ☎ 09–2253529
- 🚇 Veldstraat

Music Mania

Three floors of rock, folk, gothic, jazz and blues. Unknown artists have a short introduction so you can sometimes make a 'discovery'.

- ✉ Bagattenstraat 197
- ☎ 09–2256815
- 🚇 Zuid

De 9the Kunst

Long, narrow shop devoted to strip cartoons.

- ✉ Nederkouter 8
- ☎ 09–2240147
- 🚇 Nederkouter

De Schaar

Literature and comic strips, second-hand novelties, rare videos and imported works.

- ✉ Baudelostraat 12
- ☎ 09–2237371
- 🚇 Bij St Jacobs

Walry's

Authors in Ghent come to buy books here and present their own works in the literary café.

- ✉ Zwijnaardsesteenweg 6
- ☎ 09–2229167
- 🚇 Citadelpark

Gifts & Collector's Items

Craenkindershuys
Small shop to browse in for souvenir T-shirts, local beers and gin, and the classic tourist items. Everything to remind you of your visit to Ghent.
- ✉ **Kraanlei 2**
- ☎ **09–2243309**
- 🚋 **St Veerleplein**

Daskalides
Belgian chocolates are world famous. Not only is the factory in Ghent, there are numerous chocolate shops in the centre.
- ✉ **Henegouwenstraat 1**
- ☎ **09–2243677**
- 🚋 **Korenmarkt**

The Fallen Angel
Nude photographs from the early days of photography, old advertising posters and postcards.
- ✉ **Jan Breydelstraat 29**
- ☎ **09–2236415**
- 🚋 **St Veerleplein**

Hobby 2000
Large model shop. For anyone who wants to add Belgian trains to their collection.
- ✉ **KortrijkSepoortstraat 250**
- ☎ **09–2228820**
- 🚋 **KortrijkSepoortstraat**

Hopduvel
Huge drinks centre, ideal for anyone who would like to take home any of the 1,001 Belgian beers.
- ✉ **Coupure Left 625**
- ☎ **09–2252068**
- 🚋 **Papegaaistraat**

Interphila
Numismatists and philatelists who want to continue the hunt in Ghent must certainly visit this little shop. You can spend hours there without getting bored.
- ✉ **St Baafsplein 4**
- ☎ **09–2254680**
- 🚋 **E. Braunplein**

Peeters
They say that Belgian cheeses continue to amaze people. The manager of this shop, selling nothing but cheeses made by traditional methods, is well-known for his encyclopedic knowledge of cheese.
- ✉ **Hoornstraat 9**
- ☎ **09–2256968**
- 🚋 **Veldstraat**

Temmerman (► 74)
Antique sweetshop with long-forgotten cakes and edible flowers. Cosy shop that smells sweet and fruity.
- ✉ **Kraanlei 79**
- ☎ **09–2240041**
- 🚋 **St Veerleplein**

Tierenteyn (► 54)
Nostalgia triumphs in this old shop where the stone jars of spicy mustard will make your eyes water.
- ✉ **Groentenmarkt 3**
- ☎ **09–2258336**
- 🚋 **Korenmarkt**

Souvenirs
You will regularly see a car go past with a noose hanging on the rear-view mirror. The driver in question is a local born and bred who is as proud as a peacock about his stubborn nature. You can buy these nooses in most tourist shops and they are a morbid but original souvenir of your stay in unruly Ghent.

Children's attractions

Ghent and Children
Research has shown that people visit Ghent mainly without children. In fact it is not easy to keep young folk amused in a city that makes a great deal of its cultural heritage. The success of a holiday with children will depend to a large extent on your own ingenuity.

Blaarmeersen
This huge sports and recreation area offers many possibilities for young people. There is more than a play area for the tinies, a ski slope, scuba diving, water-skiing and sailing as well as athletics and football facilities. Many Ghent people come here in the summer to sunbathe on the little beach or for a family outing.

- ✉ **Zuiderlaan**
- ▣ **Watersportbaan**
- ⓘ **Free**

Het Fabriek
This café for children and young people makes it possible for youngsters to go out for a drink or to an event in a good atmosphere especially for them, and where parents do not have to worry about alcohol. At the weekend there are teenage discos to 7:30PM and because young people are the future, payment is entirely electronic.

- ✉ **Raffinaderijstraat 4**
- ☎ **09–2671020**
- ▣ **Krommewal**

Ghent Festivals
Anyone visiting the city after 26 July need not worry that their children will be bored in a city famous for art. For ten days there is street theatre, the children can do face painting, there are children's cafés and they will be overwhelmed with colourful impressions. In addition so much is on offer at no charge that you could probably not find a cheaper cultural and child-friendly holiday anywhere – if only you can find somewhere to stay.

Gravensteen (▶ 18)
A castle always fires

childrens imaginations. Children will probably enjoy the knights' hall, the collection of armour, the keep, and the dungeon more than their parents do. With luck there will be knights walking about the castle and drawing their swords.

Historische onderwijs-collectie
School-age children usually find it fun to see what a classroom looked like between 1900 and 1940. The scene is recreated with furniture, maps, blackboards and chalks.

- ✉ **Apotheekstraat 1**
- ☎ **09–2240224**
- ⓘ **Wed 2–4. Closed during holidays** ⓘ **£**
- ▣ **Bijloke**

Hortusmuseum Michel Thiery
This museum is specially designed for children and is also known as the 'school museum'. You learn about the natural world in a way that appeals to children. Stuffed animals, a collection of butterflies and gruesome corpses preserved in spirit put theory into practice.

- ✉ **St Pietersplein 14**
- ☎ **09–2447373**
- ⓘ **Mon–Sat 9–12:15 and 1:30–5:15** ⓘ **£**
- ▣ **St Pietersplein**

Illuseum
Actually the museum of illusion. You are initiated into the world of conjuring tricks. Most tricks involve optical illusions. Attentive visitors can work out how on earth it is possible to pull a rabbit out of a hat. Opening times vary and Illuseum is often hired by schools. Since it is a little

way out of the centre it is advisable to telephone before setting off.

✉ **Victor BraeckMonnlaan 123**
☎ **09–2282856**
🚊 **Dampoort**

Kuip van Gent (► 20)

Children always enjoy a boat trip on the Leie and Lieve rivers, particularly as on the the way they see the Gravensteen from below.

🚢 **De bootjes van Gent**
✉ **Korenlei (Groen huisje)**
☎ **09–2238853**
🕐 **Apr–Nov: Mon–Sun 10–7**
🚊 **Korenmarkt**

De Onvrije Schipper (► 38)

You do not need to miss out on going to a pub simply because your children find it difficult to sit still. This exotic pub in an historic building has a play area with colouring books and building bricks, and is the most child-friendly in the city.

✉ **Korenlei 7A**
☎ **09–2336045**
🚊 **Korenmarkt**

Paardenkoetsen (Horse-drawn Carriage Rides)

Parents who take their offspring on a boat trip through the city sometimes underestimate the skill of the skipper and like to see their children sitting at the wheel of a boat. They can avoid being disappointed by taking a carriage ride through the historic city centre instead. Children are allowed in front beside the coachman and perhaps to hold the reins. Daily from April to October from the St Baafsplein.

Pierke Pierlala (► 112)

Nonsense puppet theatre in local dialect.

S.M.A.K. (► 25)

We leave aside whether or not this is an indication of quality, but it seems that in practice children get on better with contemporary art than adults do. Certainly in this museum where are a number of interactive works on show which appeal to the inquisitive mind.

Vizit

Since 1995 the independent association Vizit vzw has been proving that guided tours need not be dry as dust or boring ways of passing the time. Through walking dinners, castle routes, theatre walks and other alternative ways of approaching the city from an original angle these enthusiastic and multilingual guides reveal the fascinating secrets of Ghent. They succeed in an animated way in catching children's attention with what looks to some like hard historical facts. You are advised to book several weeks in advance because of Vizit's success so that only those who read this guide before they leave home can be sure of taking part in one of the tours.

✉ **Kapucijnenham 9**
☎ **09–2337689**

The Zone

Enjoyment for all ages. You can play war games on a splendidly laid out court. Harmless lasers have to be avoided. The computer keeps a careful tally of which warriors have made the most kills.

✉ **Voskenslaan 135**
☎ **09–2206606**
🚊 **St Pietersstation**

Childminding

The city offers various forms of childminding: crèches, day nurseries, foster families. To find out if there are places available or for further information:
☎ **09–2343316:**

Classical Music & Theatre

Tickets

The central sales point for nearly all tickets is **Free Time vzw**. You can find the office in **Kammerstraat 19**, or can telephone on **09–2337788**. They can tell you what is happening on stage during your stay in Ghent.

🕐 Mon–Fri 10–5

Arca

This small theatre started in the experimental years of the 1950s and has found a fantastic location on the banks of the Leie.

✉ St Widowstraat 3
☎ 09–2251860
🚇 St Veerleplein

Bijloke

This festival hall recently underwent a massive facelift, the acoustics were improved and it attracts many classical orchestras with an international reputation.

✉ Jozef Kluyskensstraat
☎ 09–2257780
🚇 Martelaarslaan

Europees Figurentheatercentrum

Ghent is the European capital of puppet theatre. In this building you can not only see a performance but can catch a glimpse of the workshops and see how the puppets are made.

✉ Trommelstraat 1
☎ 09–2331215
🚇 St Veerleplein

Gele zaal

Stages mainly musical forms from all over the world: ethno-jazz, flamenco, etc.

✉ Nonnemeersstraat 26
☎ 09–2234080
🚇 Groot-Brittaniëlaan

Kopergieterij

A very young theatre that invites many foreign theatre companies, puts on childrens productions, and can be very experimental.

✉ Blekerijstraat 50
☎ 09–2337000
🚇 Kongostraat

Minard

Beautiful theatre, once the home of the Ghent Folk Theatre, now mainly Flemish and Dutch top productions.

✉ Walpoortstraat 15
☎ 09–2336468 🚇 Zuid

Nederlands Toneel Gent

This is the home of the biggest theatre company in Flanders. You usually find the classical repertoire here.

✉ St Baafsplein 17
☎ 09–2253208
🚇 E. Braunplein

Pierke Pierlala

The 'Pirandello' of Ghent. This doll makes your Wednesday or Saturday afternoon unforgettably amusing if you understand the local dialect.

✉ Kraanlei 65 ☎ 09–2231366
🚇 St Veerleplein

Sabbattini

One of the oldest and smallest pantomime theatres in Europe. A nice alternative for anyone visiting Ghent who wants to go to the theatre but whose Dutch is not very good.

✉ Burgstraat 24
☎ 09–2255515
🚇 Burgstraat

De Vlaamse Opera

An exquisite opera house behind an enormous, ugly and badly maintained facade. For big performances seating is erected on St Baafsplein and you can see everything live on a big screen.

✉ Schouwburgstraat 3
☎ 09–2252425 🚇 Kouter

Vooruit (► 71)

The temple of the arts in Ghent. All kinds of music and drama are on offer.

✉ St Pietersnieuwstraat 23
☎ 09–2255643 🚇 Zuid

Live Music

Charlatan
This was once the liveliest café in the city but the emergence of fringe establishments has eaten away at its reputation. But on Thursday evenings you can still listen to authentic hearty rock.

⊠ **Vlasmarkt 6** ☎ **09–224231**
🚊 **Bij St Jacobs**

Damberd Jazzcafé
Traditional pub with live jazz every Thursday evening, often a band of world stature. The house motto can be read out in one breath from the menu: 'shutupwhenthemusiciansplay'.

⊠ **Korenmarkt 19**
☎ **09–3295337** 🚊 **Korenmarkt**

Democrazy
Famous music club with a great nose for everything that is both new and going to last.

⊠ **Skaldenstraat 56 (Gent-Zeehaven)** ☎ **09–2232227**
🚊 **Haven**

Het Fabriek
Young people's pub with a huge climbing wall inside and where you can only pay electronically. Puts on rock and experimental chill-out.

⊠ **Raffinaderijstraat 4**
☎ **09–2671020** 🚊 **Krommewal**

Finnegan's
Belongs to a chain promoting Irish drink and music as part of the human world heritage. There's a jolly and friendly crowd here.

⊠ **Hooiaard 8** ☎ **09–2341984**
🚊 **Korenmarkt**

Fnac
This book and record shop offers its customers performances every day. Big and small names come here to promote their latest book or CD.

⊠ **Veldstraat 88** ☎ **09–2234080**
🚊 **Veldstraat**

Lazy River Jazz Club
In this pub every Friday evening you are reminded that the inventor of the saxophone was familiar with Ghent.

⊠ **Stadhuissteeg 5**
☎ **09–2304139**
🚊 **E. Braunplein**

Het Magazijn
Trendy pub cum brasserie, music hall every Friday, and a free concert every Saturday which allows the DJs to show off their talent.

⊠ **Penitentenstraat 24**
☎ **09–2340708**
🚊 **Bij St Jacobs**

De Onvrije Schipper
On Thursday evenings this beautiful but tiny cellar pub throbs to Spanish and Latin-American sounds.

⊠ **Korenlei 7** ☎ **09–2336045**
🚊 **Korenmarkt**

Trefpunt
To prove Monday does not need to be dull the most important organiser of the Ghent Festival brings in a band. Often a Dutch and socially-committed repertoire.

⊠ **St Jacobs 18**
☎ **09–2253676**
🚊 **Bij St Jacobs**

Urga
In this café with a Russian theme Russia is the order of the day: the drink, the snacks and the music. There are Russian songs almost every day or you can listen to Russian folk music.

⊠ **Kartuizerlaan 105**
☎ **09–2252945** 🚊 **Tolhuislaan**

Thursday Evening Events
To judge from the diary of events, the city is at its liveliest on Thursday evenings. Most pubs have a fixed day for live music performances but this applies only from October to June. During the summer there is too much music already on offer for the management to go on investing in musicians.

Sport

Sport and Recreation Office

Lovers of sport are well catered for in this city both as participants and spectators. The Sport and Recreation Office supplies all kinds of information about sports facilities. You can find information on times of opening, lessons and the various activities on offer direct from the Sport and Recreation Office during normal office hours.

⊠ Zuiderlaan 5
☎ 09–2438880
◑ 10–5

AA Gent

This is without a doubt the most successful of the many football teams in Ghent. It has been in the Belgian premiership for decades. The supporters club 'Buffalo' is one of the liveliest in the country; it has a training centre for cheerleaders and hires out the girls to other clubs. AA Gent is unique in the Belgian football league: in the 1950s the club made the first foreign transfer and in 1999 had the distinction of having a team without a single Belgian. Going to a match can be fun.

⊠ Tennisstraat 13 (Gentbrugge)
☎ 09–2306686
🚋 Gentbrugge

Blaarmeersen (▶ 88)

Nowhere else in the city will you find so many sports facilities together: a water-sports course, ski slope, athletics tracks, fitness circuit, football pitches, mountain bike circuit, practice pool for deep-sea divers, multi gyms and a Finnish track for joggers.

⊠ Zuiderlaan ☎ 09–2247222
🚋 Watersportbaan

Cano Club Gent vzw

There are plenty of opportunities for canoes and kayaks in this riverside city. You can combine travel and sightseeing along Coupure, Graslei and the Lieve.

⊠ Yachtdreef 1
☎ 09–2226657
🚋 Watersportbaan

Elite

Fitness salon, bodybuilding, power training and cardio aerobics. Advice is always available if you ask.

⊠ Zwijnaardsesteenweg 227

Evergreen Snookerpalace

Large snooker salon in a peaceful, British atmosphere.

⊠ Sleepstraat 74
☎ 09–2241700 🚋 Sleepstraat

Jan Yoens

The only open-air swimming pool in the city, apart from lakes and ponds.

⊠ Dracenastraat 8
☎ 09–2262872 🚋 Wondelgem

Kristallijn

Large skating rink with speed track and disco area. During the Christmas period the fanatical skater can skate in the open air below the Belfort.

⊠ Warmoezeniersweg 20
☎ 09–2221010 🚋 Kristallijn

De Maybloem

Very large bowling alley where both professionals and amateurs immediately feel at home. The scoring and provision of the pins are computer controlled.

⊠ Maybloemstraat 18
☎ 09–2272772 🚋 Brugse Poort

Stadium

The place for indoor sports: climbing wall, squash, billiards, aerobics, badminton, mini-football, volleyball and ball pool for the children.

⊠ Waalsekrook
☎ 09–2661893
🚋 Zuid

Van Eyck

This municipal swimming pool that is also used as a film set is visited as a unique piece of architecture as well as by water fanatics.

⊠ Jules De Vigneplein 5
☎ 09–2259629
🚋 Oude Beestenmarkt

Miscellaneous

Carillon Concerts
At intervals you can hear the following beautiful pieces of music played on the carillon in the Belfort (▶ 32).

On the hour you can enjoy *Vrede van Madrid*.

At quarter past the hour the bells play *Gavotte* by the composer Jean Baptiste Loeillet.

On the half hour it is the turn of the *Scherensliep*.

At quarter to the hour if you are near the bell tower you can hear *Op den Slagh van Paria*.

Every Sunday morning at 11:30AM there is a concert from the bell tower.

Fishing
The Coupure and Blaarmeersen are favourite places for the keen fisherman. In Belgium as in many European countries you need a permit to fish and you can obtain this from a post office for a small payment. After that you can relax with your fellow fishermen by the water and enjoy the surroundings after your many excursions through beautiful Ghent.

Jazz in the Park
On Fridays every year during August jazz concerts are held in the Zuiderpark in Ghent in both afternoon and evening and these are free. You can enjoy performances of the real jazz classics.

Koisk Concerts
A series of concerts for wind and band music held in the flower market on the Kouter, performed by the best brass bands in Ghent. You can hear the concerts from May to the end of September.

Sauna
The therapy part of the Strop swimming pool has an oxygen sauna, sunbed, ventilated outdoor room, ice-cold plunge pool, massage parlour and a rest room with a pleasant sitting area. You can also swim in the pool.
- ✉ **Stropstraat 31**
- ☎ **09-2213373**
- ⏰ **Mon–Sat 1:30 and Sun 9–12:30**

Son et Lumière 'Ghent and Emperor Charles'
In the School Museum part of Ghent's history is told using a model that shows the city as it was 450 years ago at the time of Emperor Charles V. *Son et Lumière* performances (in Dutch) take place at 11AM and 3PM. From Monday to Thursday inclusive and on Saturday the museum is open 9AM to 12:15PM and 1:30PM to 5:15PM. On Friday the museum is open only in the morning and it is closed on Sunday.

Sporthal Vlaanderen
Athletics, aerobics, badminton, basketball, gymnastics, handball, judo, mini-football, fencing, Tae Kwon-do, table tennis, tennis, volleyball, indoor football and much more. This is a paradise for those keen on sport.

Nightclubs
There are plenty of nightclubs in the city but you will be refused entry unless you have a membership card. If you want to experience a more spicy and erotic nightlife, you can visit the red-light district between Brabantdam and St Annaplein.

What's on When

January
Large antiques fair in the buildings of St Pietersabdij.

Lent
Opening of the Belgian fair season on St Pietersplein.

April
An enormous exhibition with the intriguing name *Flanders Technology* (only takes place in years divisible by three).

End of April/Beginning of May
Every five years Ghent lives up to its title as a flower city during the Ghent *Floraliën*, a large-scale exhibition of house and garden plants and many, many flowers. In the 2000 event, theme gardens were also introduced. Sheer enjoyment of colours and scents.
✉ **Flanders Expo, St Denijs Westrem**
☎ **09–2419211 or 09–2415099**
🕐 **Every five years in the last week of April. Next exhibition is planned to take place in 2005.**

Whitsuntide
International jazz festival. Performances here and there in the city and jazz pub crawls. Every lover of jazz has got to experience it once.

11 July
Flemish National Day. Free rock performances throughout the city. Friendliness, meetings and beer are high on the agenda on this Ghent occasion.

End of July
The Ghent Festival. The biggest cultural folk festival in Europe. Held annually in the second half of July. A multicultural festival lasting ten days and almost completely free.
A collection of street theatre, cultural debate about society, youth happenings, fair and open-air spectaculars. The list is supplemented by cabaret, concerts, fireworks, sculpture on the inland waterways, music and all this many times over – this gives you some idea what the festival includes.

September/October
Festival of Flanders. Beautiful, classical music of the highest level performed at various locations in the city. An absolute must for lovers of classical composers.

First Sunday in October
Open Building Day. Various buildings throughout the city that are normally closed to visitors, can be seen without charge.

Beginning of October
International Flanders-Ghent Film Festival. New films are shown.

Christmas Period
Jolly Christmas market and skating rink below the Belfort. Helps you get into the mood and buy all kinds of things to decorate your house for Christmas.

Practical Matters

Above: *a pleasant pavement café in Ostend*
Right: *local people do not like the average letterbox*

TIME DIFFERENCES

GMT
12 noon

Belgium
1PM

British Summer
1PM

Netherlands
1PM

USA (NY)
7AM

USA (LA)
4AM

BEFORE YOU GO

WHAT YOU NEED

		Belgium	Netherlands	Germany	UK	USA
●	Required					
○	Suggested					
▲	Not required					
Passport/National Identity Card		●	●	●	●	●
Visa		▲	▲	▲	▲	▲
Onward or Return Ticket		▲	○	○	○	○
Health Inoculations		▲	▲	▲	▲	▲
Health Documentation (► Health, 123)		▲	●	●	●	●
Travel Insurance		○	○	○	○	○
Driving Licence (national)		●	●	●	●	●
Green Card (if own car)		▲	●	●	●	●
Car Registration Document (if own car)		▲	●	●	●	●

WHEN TO GO

Ghent

▓▓▓ High season

▢▢▢ Low season

3°C	6°C	10°C	13°C	19°C	21°C	23°C	22°C	18°C	14°C	8°C	6°C
JAN	FEB	MAR	APR	MAY	JUN	JUL	AUG	SEP	OCT	NOV	DEC
☀	☁	☁	⛅	☀	☀	☀	☀	☀	☁	☁	☁

☁ Wet   ☁ Cloudy   ☀ Sun   ⛅ Sun/showers

TOURIST OFFICES

In the UK
Belgian Tourist Office
29 Princes Street
London W1R 7RG
☎ 0900–1887799

Tourism Flanders
31 Pepper Street
London E14 9RW
☎ 020 7867 0311

In the USA
Suite 1501
780 Third Avenue
New York NY 10017
☎ 212–7588130

POLICE 101

FIRE 100

AMBULANCE 100

WHEN YOU ARE THERE

ARRIVING

If you arrive by air you will land at Zaventem International (Brussels). Four trains an hour run to Brugge-Centraal. From there you can take a train to St Pietersstation. You can also take the very slow stopping train from the airport that leaves once an hour for St Pietersstation. British visitors can take Eurostar to Brussels, then a local train to Ghent. If you arrive by train it is better to get off at St Pietersstation than at Gent-Dampoort Station.

There are enough taxis at the station to take you and your luggage to the hotel or you can travel more cheaply by tram 1, 10, 11, 12, 13, 21, 22 or 40.

Zaventem Airport Kilometres to Ghent	Journey times	
	🚆	0.45 hours
65km	🚌	1.30 hours
	🚗	1.00 hours

MONEY

The unit of currency is the euro but until December 2001, the Belgian franc will continue to be used. A dual pricing system will operate. In January 2002 euro bank notes and coins will replace the Belgian franc which will cease to be legal tender in July 2002. Euro notes come in denominations of 10, 20, 50, 100, 200 and 500 and coins in denominations of 1, 2, 5, 10, 20 and 50 centimes, 1 and 2 euros.

TIME

 Belgium follows Central European Time (CET) which is one hour ahead of Greenwich Mean Time (GMT+1), but from the end of March to the end of October it is on summertime (GMT+2).

CUSTOMS

 YES

From a non-EU country for personal use:
Cigarettes: 200 or
Tobacco: 250 grams
Spirits : 1 litre or
Fortified wine (sherry, port): 2 litres
Wine: 2 litres

From an EU country for personal use (guidelines):
Cigarettes: 800 or
Tobacco: 1 kilogram
Spirits: 10 litres or
Fortified wine: 20 litres
Wine: 90 litres
Beer: 110 litres

 NO

Drugs, firearms, explosives, offensive weapons, protected animal species.

EMBASSIES (IN BRUSSELS)

UK	USA	Australia	Canada
02–2876211	02–5082111	02–2310500	02–7410611

IN GHENT

TOURIST OFFICES

Ghent

- **Tourism Ghent**
  Belfort
  Botermarkt 17a
  9000 Ghent
  ☎ 09 225 3641
  Supplies information
  leaflets, street plans,
  events diaries and can
  book guided tours.

- **Tourist Board East
  Flanders**
  W. Wilsonplein 3
  9000 Ghent
  ☎ 09 267 7117
  Helpful office if you would
  like to see more of the
  Province of East Flanders.

Brussels

- **Flanders Tourist
  Commission**
  Grasmarkt 61
  1000 Brussels
  ☎ 02 504 0300

- **Touring Club of Belgium**
  Wetstraat 44
  1040 Brussels
  ☎ 02 233 2211

- **Toerisme Vlaanderen**
  Grasmarkt 63
  1000 Brussels
  ☎ 02 504 0390

Antwerp

- **Tourism Antwerp**
  Grotemarkt 15
  2000 Antwerp
  ☎ 03 232 0103

Bruges

- **Tourism Bruges**
  Burg 11
  Bruges
  ☎ 05 044 8686

NATIONAL HOLIDAYS

J	F	M	A	M	J	J	A	S	O	N	D
1		(1)	(1)	1(2)	(2)	(2)	(1)	1		2	1

1 Jan	New Year's Day
Mar/Apr	Easter Monday
1 May	May Day
May/Jun	Ascension Day
May/Jun	Whit Monday
11 Jul	Flemish National Day
21 Jul	Belgian National Day
15 Aug	Assumption
27 Sep	Walloon National Day
1 Nov	All Saints' Day
11 Nov	Armistice Day
25 Dec	Christmas Day

Most shops, banks and offices are closed on these
days. The Flemish and Walloon National Days are not
official holidays but they are generally celebrated.

OPENING TIMES

○ Shops ● Post Offices
● Offices ● Museums
● Banks ● Pharmacies

Pharmacies have a night and weekend rota which is
displayed on the door of all pharmacies when they
are closed.

Shops and banks are closed on public holidays,
except on 15 November. If this holiday falls on a
Sunday you can expect everything to be closed the
next day. Flemish National Day applies only to
Flanders. Walloon National Day is 27 September.

DRIVE ON THE RIGHT

TOILETS NOT FREE

PUBLIC TRANSPORT

Trains Belgium has the densest railway network in the world. Although the trains cannot always be said to be punctual and tickets are expensive you can get to all parts of the country easily by train.

Anyone under 26 who plans to travel regularly should buy a Go-pass. Senior citizens too enjoy a welcome reduction. You can catch most trains at St Pietersstation (Maria Hendrikplein).

Tram and bus All parts of the city centre are served by trams or buses between 5AM and 11PM. The three most important stops are the W.Wilsonplein, Korenmarkt and St Pietersstation. You will also find shops there where you can buy tram or bus tickets and where you find information about the various tariffs. Information ☎ 09–2109491

Shopping shuttle bus This runs on Saturdays and on Sundays in the Christmas shopping period, between 12 noon and 7PM, a free bus between parking 8 at Flanders Expo and the centre of Ghent. The bus runs every ten minutes and both it and the parking are free. Info: 09–2667761

Cycle Hire There are several places to hire cycles. One of them is St Pietersstation (09–2412224). Anyone who knows how many stolen bikes are fished out of the Leie and the Coupure each year will understand that a cycle lock is an absolute necessity. Many local people ride a bike that costs less than their cycle lock.

CAR RENTAL

The major car rental firms have free phone numbers (0800–), and you can find the details in in *De Gouden Gids* (*Yellow Pages*). Generally you need to have had four years' experience. The prices are fairly reasonable.

TAXIS

The biggest and best-known firm in Ghent is V-Tax (09–2222222). A trip from the station to the city centre costs about BF350. Between 10PM and 6AM there is a small surcharge. Tips are included in the price.

DRIVING

Maximum speed limits on motorways: **120 kph**. Mimimum: **90 kph**

Speed limit on all main roads: **90 kph**.

Speed limit in built-up areas: **50 kph**. 'Zone 30' streets: **30 kph**.

Front and rear seat belts are mandatory.

Blood alcohol limit: 0.5%. Random breath tests are made regularly.

The centre of Ghent is car free! Do not be misled if you see vehicles in the historic centre – they belong to trades people or residents. If you dare to drive or park there the cost will be steep.

Vehicles parked in the wrong place are towed away without warning to a pound 20km outside Ghent. The cost of the tow truck, your transport to the pound, and the fine will come to around BF8,000. It is thus advisable to put sufficient coins in the parking meter or (an expensive business) use an underground car park.

SAFETY

Ghent is a fairly peaceful city and has a good reputation for safety. However, some precautions are advisable.

- Avoid the Citadelpark after dark.
- Look after your handbag; there are always pickpockets in the shopping streets.
- Ghent is a multicultural city, but there is an extreme right element which occasionally rears its ugly head.
- The police operate on bicycles in the traffic-free part of the city.

Police assistance
☎ **101**
from any telephone box

TELEPHONES

Coin operated telephones have become a rarity although you can still find them in some pubs. Usually you need a phone card that is obtainable from newsagents and post offices. Some charge cards can also be used. The code for Ghent is 09, be careful, you always need to dial this number.

International Dialling Codes	
From Belgium to:	
UK:	**00 44**
Ireland:	**00 353**
USA/Canada:	**00 1**
Netherlands:	**00 31**
Australia:	**00 61**
Germany:	**00 49**

Information on foreign codes is available on: 1224. Mon–Fri 6PM–8AM. All day at weekends and holidays the tariff is cheaper.

POST

In recent years a lot of post offices have disappeared so you have to walk a long way to find a stamp.

The head post office is at Stapelplein 75.

ELECTRICITY

In Belgium the power supply is 220 volts AC. Plugs are round with two pins. British appliances will need an adaptor. For most non-European equipment you will also need a transformer to 100–120 volts AC.

TIPS/GRATUITIES

Yes ✓ No ✗		
Restaurants	✗	
Hotels (chambermaids, porters)	✗	
Bars	✗	
Doormen in discos	✓	BF50
Taxis	✗	
Guides	✓	As you please
Cloakroom attendants	✓	BF10–20
Toilets	✓	BF10–20
Hairdressers	✓	BF50

PHOTOGRAPHY

People in Ghent do not find being photographed in the street unusual. There are various art academies in the city and students regularly have projects to shoot portraits. This does not means that pushiness is appreciated, it is better to ask someone's permission before photographing him or her. The best light for photography is in November.

You can buy **film** at the pharmacy, in supermarkets, souvenir shops and, of course, in a camera shop or opticians.

HEALTH

Health insurance

Within the EU there are agreements about the payment of medical costs for visitors from other member states but not all risks are covered. For example, you will need extra insurance to cover dental treatment. Ask your travel insurer what cover you need for Belgium. Credit cards may provide some insurance cover. Non-EU visitors need full medical cover.

Dentist

Make sure that your medical insurance covers dental treatment.

Protection from the sun

The early sun (May, June) can be treacherous and a sun cream will protect you from being chapped by the wind. Asthma patients should stay indoors in good weather because of the high ozone concentration. Midges are a summer problem in Ghent and you can buy slow-burning tablets in the supermarkets against these little pests.

Medicines

If you take medicines regularly take them with you and a doctor's note to avoid problems at Customs. You can phone 0900–10500 to find out which pharmacist is on duty. Most medicines are not obtainable without a prior visit to the doctor.

Safe drinking water

Although tap water is generally safe and drunk by most locals, some areas have rust in the mains and there is a lot of lime in the water. Mineral water is cheap and easily obtainable. If you ask for a glass of water in a café or restaurant, you will be served mineral water and expected to pay for it.

CONCESSIONS

You can take advantage of reductions for many attractions. Children, senior citizens, students, widows, orphans, the disabled and unemployed are often eligible for reductions if they produce their passports and a proof of status.

CLOTHING SIZES

UK	USA	Belgium /Europe	
36	36	46	
38	38	48	
40	40	50	
42	42	52	Suits
44	44	54	
46	46	56	
7	8	41	
7.5	8.5	42	
8.5	9.5	43	
9.5	10.5	44	Shoes
10.5	11.5	45	
11	12	46	
14.5	14.5	37	
15	15	38	
15.5	15.5	39/40	
16	16	41	Shirts
16.5	16.5	42	
17	17	43	
8	6	34	
10	8	36	
12	10	38	
14	12	40	Dresses
16	14	42	
18	16	44	
4.5	6	38	
5	6.5	38	
5.5	7	39	
6	7.5	39	Shoes
6.5	8	40	
7	8.5	41	

WHEN DEPARTING

- It is usual to confirm the return flight. Make it easy for yourself and do it on arrival.
- If you arrive at the airport less than an hour and a half before your flight your seat may have been sold.
- Taxis as well as trains go to the airport from Ghent. It is better to book one, on 09–2521832. Prices are reasonable.

LANGUAGE

Dutch is the official language of Flanders. Most young inhabitants of Antwerp also speak English, whilst the older ones speak French. The Antwerp dialect itself is alive and kicking, although tourists are not expected to speak it.

Not everybody speaks English, though, making it useful to know some Dutch words, and attempts to use them will be appreciated. The 'oo' (pronounced 'oa' as in load) and 'ee' constructions (pronounced 'ay' as in day) are particularly problematic for English-speakers. If you pronounce 'ij' like English 'eye' you'll be close enough: for example *prijs* 'price'; *ontbijt* 'ontbite'.

hotel	*hotel*	breakfast	*ontbijt*
room	*kamer*	toilet	*toilet/WC*
single/	*eenpersoonskamer/*	bathroom	*badkamer*
double	*tweepersoonskamer*	shower	*douche*
one/two nights	*een/twee nachten*	balcony	*balkon*
per person/	*per persoon/*	key	*sleutel*
per room	*per kamer*	room service	*room service*
reservation	*reservering*	chambermaid	*kamermeisje*
rate	*prijs*		

bank	*bank*	American dollar	*Amerikaanse dollar*
exchange office	*wisselkantoor*	banknote	*papiergeld*
post office	*postkantoor*	coin	*wisselgeld/kleingeld*
cashier	*kassa*	credit card	*creditcard*
foreign exchange	*buitenlands geld*	traveller's cheque	*reischeque*
currency	*valuta*	exchange rate	*wisselkoers*
British pound	*Engels/Britse pond*	commission charge	*commissie*

restaurant	*restaurant*	starter	*voorgerecht*
café	*café*	main course	*hoofdgerecht*
table	*tafel*	dish of the day	*dagschotel*
menu	*menukaart*	dessert	*nagerecht*
set menu	*menu*	drink	*drank/drankje*
wine list	*wijnkaart*	waiter	*ober*
lunch	*lunch/middageten*	waitress	*serveerster*
dinner	*diner/avondeten*	the bill	*de rekening*

aeroplane	*vliegtuig*	single/return	*enkele reis/retour*
airport	*luchthaven*	first/	*eerste klas/*
train	*trein*	second class	*tweede klas*
station	*station*	ticket office	*boekingskantoor*
bus	*bus*	timetable	*dienstregeling*
station	*busstation*	seat	*plaats*
ferry	*veerboot*	non-smoking	*niet roken*
port	*haven*	reserved	*gereserveerd*
ticket	*reisekaart*	taxi!	*taxi!*

yes	*ja*	help!	*help!*
no	*nee*	today	*vandaag*
please	*alstublieft*	tomorrow	*morgen*
thank you	*dank u*	yesterday	*gisteren*
hello	*dag/hallo*	how much?	*hoeveel?*
goodbye	*dag/tot ziens*	expensive	*duur*
goodnight	*welterusten*	closed	*gesloten*
sorry	*excuseer/pardon*	open	*geopend*

INDEX

Acknowledgements
The publishers would like to thank the following photographers and libraries for their assistance in the preparation of this book:

ARMAND VERSPEETEN 26, 38, BELGACOM 122a, DIENST VOOR TOERISME AALST 78, DIENST VOOR TOERISME BRUGGE 80, 81, DIENST VOOR TOERISME GENT 1, 5a, 9, 10b, 11, 15a, 18, 32, 44, 60, 64, 66, 69, 70, G. OP HET VELD 52a, 52b, 72, 76, 77, 84, 85, 86, 87, 89, 90, 117a, 117b, 122c, POLITIE ANTWERPEN 122b, JEROEN VAN DER SPEK 2, 25, 37, 50, 53, TEO VAN GERWEN DESIGN 5b, 6, 7, 8, 10a, 12, 13, 14, 19, 20, 21, 22, 23, 24, 27a, 29, 33, 34, 35, 36a, 36b, 39, 40, 41, 42, 43, 45, 46, 47, 48, 49, 51, 54a, 54b, 55a, 55b, 56, 57, 58, 59, 61, 63a, 63b, 65, 67a, 67b, 68, 71, 73, 74, 75, 83, 91a, 91b TOERISME ANTWERPEN 82, **TOERISME VLAANDEREN**: D. DE KIEVITH 27b, J. DE BRIE 62, T. OVL 9b, TOERISME VLAANDEREN 15b, 16-17, 88, W. SIEMOENS 28

Dear Essential Traveller

Your comments, opinions and recommendations are very important to us. So please help us to improve our travel guides by taking a few minutes to complete this simple questionnaire.

You do not need a stamp (unless posted outside the UK). If you do not want to cut this page from your guide, then photocopy it or write your answers on a plain sheet of paper.

Send to: **The Editor, AA World Travel Guides, FREEPOST SCE 4598, Basingstoke RG21 4GY.**

Your recommendations...

We always encourage readers' recommendations for restaurants, nightlife or shopping – if your recommendation is used in the next edition of the guide, we will send you a *FREE* AA *Essential* Guide of your choice. Please state below the establishment name, location and your reasons for recommending it.

_____

_____

_____

_____

Please send me **AA *Essential*** _____
(*see list of titles inside the front cover*)

About this guide...

Which title did you buy?
   AA *Essential* _____
Where did you buy it? _____
When? m m / y y

Why did you choose an AA *Essential* Guide? _____

_____

_____

_____

_____

Did this guide meet your expectations?
   Exceeded ☐ Met all ☐ Met most ☐ Fell below ☐
   Please give your reasons_____

_____

_____

_____

continued on next page...

Were there any aspects of this guide that you particularly liked? _____

_____

_____

_____

Is there anything we could have done better? _____

_____

_____

_____

_____

About you…

Name (*Mr/Mrs/Ms*) _____

    Address _____

_____

_____ Postcode _____

    Daytime tel nos _____

Which age group are you in?

    Under 25 ☐ 25–34 ☐ 35–44 ☐ 45–54 ☐ 55–64 ☐ 65+ ☐

How many trips do you make a year?

    Less than one ☐ One ☐ Two ☐ Three or more ☐

Are you an AA member? Yes ☐ No ☐

About your trip…

When did you book? m m / y y   When did you travel? m m / y y

How long did you stay? _____

Was it for business or leisure? _____

Did you buy any other travel guides for your trip?

    If yes, which ones? _____

_____

Thank you for taking the time to complete this questionnaire. Please send
it to us as soon as possible, and remember, you do not need a stamp
(*unless posted outside the UK*).

Happy Holidays!